the MANLEY

m e m o i r s

the MANLEY

m e m o i r s

Beverley Manley

Ian Randle Publishers
Kingston   Miami

Published in Jamaica, 2008 by
Ian Randle Publishers
11 Cunningham Avenue
Box 686, Kingston 6
www.ianrandlepublishers.com

National Library of Jamaica Cataloguing-in-Publication Data

Manley, Beverley
    The Manley memoirs / Beverley Manley

    p. : ill. ; cm

  ISBN 978-976-637-313-9 (pbk)

1. Manley, Beverley – Autobiography 2. Manley, Michael, 1924 – 1997
3. Jamaica – Politics and government 4. Jamaica – Social life and customs

I. Title

920 - dc 22

Cover and Book design by Ian Randle Publishers
Printed in the United States of America

*This book is dedicated to the many Jamaicans who
have sacrificed so that their fellow citizens
can one day live in prosperity*

Preface

That the Jamaica Labour Party government chose February 29 in 1972, for the country's general elections always intrigued Michael Manley's mother, Edna, for it was also her birthday. Edna Manley was a deeply intuitive person and sensed — quite rightly as it turned out — that victory would be ours.

We in the People's National Party (PNP) had worked continuously since 1969 to win those elections, and it was during those three years that I grew to know Michael Manley, the man who would become prime minister, the man who would become my husband. As we travelled every inch of the island together on campaign tours, I came to understand firsthand, in a way I had not previously, aspects of the culture and politics of Jamaica. Michael and I came from different worlds, economically and socially, but we were convinced that we could teach each other about those worlds, and that we could make a difference, particularly for the poor and the marginalised.

But we were naïve. We underestimated what it would take to change the power balance in Jamaican society. We underestimated, too, what it would take to balance the power within our relationship. As we set out on a life together, we could not know that it would evolve along a path of love, infidelity, betrayal, and life-changing events on a national and international scale.

Early in my marriage to Michael, the person I became was the woman I thought he wanted me to be. I fooled myself that

I was fiercely independent, when in fact I was constantly operating under his umbrella. Later, I would seek to be what the left wing of the party wanted me to be.

Though my story played out on a very public stage, to some extent my experience mirrors that of every woman struggling to maintain her identity while supporting her husband in his search for fulfilment. As a mother, political activist, academic and media personality, I have performed many roles and taken on many responsibilities, including some that no one else wanted. I did what I thought was expected of me.

My personal relationship with Michael unfolded during the crisis-ridden and violent political events of the 1970s. In an atmosphere that left us feeling constantly under attack, 'political' and 'personal' became inseparable. I subsumed my needs into the larger struggle — into Michael's vision of justice and equality. In the beginning I felt a measure of satisfaction, particularly when I saw some results of my actions and my leadership in the women's movement. The US civil rights movement was in full swing and elements of it had spilled over into Jamaica. The second wave of feminism was resulting in a consciousness-raising revolution as our women began to see themselves in a different light, and thus became more determined to play a broader role in society. The time was ripe for militant leadership of the kind I would bring to the PNP Women's Movement. Gradually I came to recognise the allure and seduction of politics, as exciting as it was challenging.

In 1980, however, the dream would be shattered. With the PNP's massive defeat in the general elections, I lost my way. By that time I had also lost my identity and it was time to reclaim it. Alone, I embarked upon another stage of my journey, one that entailed a struggle for survival — psychological, economic and political. I experienced rejection, both personal and public, because I had dared, as a woman, to make decisions about my own life, because I had dared to leave the Great Man. But I had come to realize that leaving was the only way I would survive. I had to survive. And I did.

But my story begins many years earlier. I grew up in a lower middle class home with limited resources. My mother, educated yet living a life that made her unhappy, was determined that her children would receive an education. Education, she taught us, was the only way out. My relationship with my mother was always intense and often traumatic, and I see now that it — along with my experience of the power struggle between men and women as observed first in my parents' troubled union — was largely responsible for who I was to become. For who I am.

Acknowledgements

I wish to thank the following, without whom this work would not have been possible.

Kwame Dawes, who felt I had a story to tell and who gave me invaluable support during the early part of the process by asking the right questions and keenly listening to my answers.

Diana Thorburn-Chen, who insisted that I write for the younger generation.

Professor Errol Morrison, who encouraged me to write what he recognised as an important gender story.

Rachel Manley, who at a critical part of the process, stepped in and read the manuscript, loved it, and helped me to reorganise it.

My children, who encouraged me to write and never for one moment inhibited me.

D.K., who provided the space for me to do what I knew in my heart I had to do.

The CHASE Fund (Jamaica), which gave me the necessary financial support for the project; Henry Lowe and Audrey Marks for their support, which included early funding; and the chairman, general manager and staff of the Jamaica Pegasus Hotel who, from time to time, provided room facilities for the writing.

Chapter 1

I woke up every morning of my childhood to the sound of Mama's complaining voice. She would shake me, hands on my shoulders, as she said fearsomely, 'Wake up, shake up.' There was always an urgency in her tone, as though she feared that if we did not get up when she told us to, we would be late for school — or worse yet, late for life. We would be imperfect children. Her words were always muttered, desperate, rhythmic and unchanging over the years. As I rose, she would continue her nagging — relentlessly her voice made its way through her body and out into an uncertain, often hostile, world in which she was both victim and conqueror. Watching and listening to my mother, Esmine Pearson Anderson, was a way of life. She worried about everything. She nagged non-stop. Life was hard for her and she was not going to let any of us forget it. What she had taken on by marrying my father was a life sentence. But she had made her bed and was prepared to lie in it.

My father was as silent as my mother was voluble. This confused me, and made me determined to answer her back, no matter what the cost.

I grew up the second of four children of my parents' marriage. My sister Shirley is two years older than me, and my sister Roma is two years younger. My brother Maurice came seven years after me so, for most of my early years, there were just the three girls.

I remember being well cared for by my mother, who did everything in the household. Occasionally she would employ a helper, but this never lasted because she believed that no one could keep the house clean the way she could. The importance of cleanliness was something I was taught to be aware of early, something I equated with the smell of Dettol disinfectant. Dishes and glasses had to be washed squeaky clean and there could be no tell-tale dried droplets on them. Every drop of water had to drain off naturally. Nothing less was acceptable. Mama would often wait until I had finished washing up, then she would calmly put everything back into the sink for me to do a second wash. I felt resentful, unable to understand why she enjoyed making me suffer.

Mama had been brought up differently from her siblings, who had been left in the care of my grandmother's sisters, the Aunts. She had been sent to secondary school at Holy Childhood, where she had been and raised as a Roman Catholic. Her siblings had gone to elementary school but had never been allowed to graduate. Mama had dreamed of being a surgeon, but that was not to be. For her, many things were not to be.

Mama seldom talked about her mother, but I always knew that she had been her father's joy. As his last child, my grandfather had spoiled her. She learned how to dress well, and she had jewellery, but he had also brought her up to be tough, to stand up for herself. She was somewhat androgynous — unafraid to display both her feminine and masculine personas at a time when it took courage to do so. She depended on no man to do any tasks. She did what she needed to do. She ended up as a housewife with four children. Though her dream of becoming a surgeon was never to be realised, she found other ways to carry out her healing functions — often tending to ill neighbours. She even created and administered her own medicines from local herbs.

My mother read a great deal, and one of the things she said about my father was that they shared a passion for books, and that when he was wooing her, he wrote her the most beautiful love letters. It is one of the few kind things she ever said about him.

My mother stayed home and performed every chore you could think of. She was the dry cleaner who took care of all my father's clothes, in particular his pinstripe suits. He was, in fact, a dapper dresser. She cleaned his shoes, brown and white, and black and white for Sundays only. She used the polish and the whitening, always being extremely careful not to let the whitening get on the black or the brown sections. She made all our clothes. She was our doctor and our dentist. In addition to toothpaste, which she mistrusted because it was too sweet and hence would rot our teeth, she insisted that we use 'chew stick', the bitter bark of a tree that we chewed and with which we massaged our gums and cleaned our teeth. It cost nothing. I did not see a dentist until I was 21 years old and had left home, yet my teeth were in excellent condition. She cooked, she baked, she cleaned — oh, how she cleaned! She worked morning, noon and night.

Mama favoured rituals, such as the 'wash-out' at the beginning of every school term. This usually meant our having to consume castor oil and herb tea, followed by Epsom salts. I had a great deal of trouble taking these medicines and had to be held down by two or three women. Even after they thought that I had swallowed it, I would bring it back up. But they would hold me down again until I gave in.

We were each assigned our own washrags and combs. We could not borrow from one another. My mother considered it unsanitary to use a towel more than once without washing it. There was a ritual with the washrags too. We had to launder them after each use and then, at the end of the week, my mother would collect and boil them in a huge pan to sterilise them. She always urged us to wear clean underwear in case we had an accident and had to be seen by a doctor, and told us never to sit on anyone else's bed. To us, the former was logical, the latter absurd. Nonetheless, we obeyed her.

When we lived in homes where we had to share the bathroom with fellow tenants, my mother always went ahead, Dettol in hand, disinfecting everything, particularly the toilet seats. Only then were we allowed to enter the bathroom and use it. Mama continued to bathe us until we were 12 years old. She did not trust us to bathe ourselves properly. By the time we came out of the bath, our skin had been rubbed red, especially inside and outside the ears. I can feel the sting even now, and the sense of being invaded when she insisted on washing my young breasts and even my vagina. Yet, I never resisted her in the bathroom. The strap — here in the form of a wet washrag — was ever ready in the case of any type of protest.

Her tyranny of cleanliness affected every aspect of our lives, even those that should have been simple childhood pleasures. I remember I particularly liked eating Bombay mangoes. I would cut the two cheeks off, suck the seed clean and then use a spoon to take care of the rest. Mama only allowed us to eat mangoes outside in the yard, and only if she tied paper bibs around our necks. I can feel the juice, sweet and sticky, running down my chin and fingers and even down my arms. I can smell the varying scents, each distinct, depending on the type of mango — Blackie, Beefie, Hairy — and finally the satisfying comfort of the mangoes deep down in my stomach. But we faced Mama's wrath if any sign of the stickiness lingered on our bodies after the feasting.

Children being children, we often got scratches and cuts at school. On our return home the first order of business was to sit on the step while our mother got to work with the bandages, Dettol and Zam-Buk — a British ointment that supposedly healed without scars. First she cleaned out the wound with the Dettol. However much this might sting, we weren't allowed to flinch or cry. She brought us up to be able to withstand pain and be strong. Tears were seen as a sign of weakness, rudeness or rebellion. I resented being shouted at and often cried with frustration — wanting to say things to her but unable to do so. This did not endear me to her, as, unlike my sisters, apart from at bath time, I never gave in to her — an attitude which often earned me a second beating.

As we grew up, our clothes and shoes were separated into church clothes, school clothes and yard clothes. We always wore Clarks shoes, imported from England and which lasted until we outgrew them. At the start I would get Shirley's and Roma would get mine. Shirley, being the eldest, would get new Clarks shoes — more expensive than the others but, in the long run, cost effective, Mama said. They were always of the same design, brown or black leather with a strap across the front that was attached by a small button. When my mother bought Clarks shoes she got exactly what she wanted: items that were consistent, reliable and practical — exactly like Mama.

Purchasing these shoes was always an event. My mother would insist that all three of us should go even if she was buying shoes only for Shirley, for there was no one to leave us at home with. These were embarrassing occasions for us girls. My mother would harass the sales clerk to the point of exasperation. The shoes had to fit properly and the sign of a good shoe was that its sole could be bent so that the toe touched the heel in as many directions as possible, without unnecessary creasing. Clarks shoes always passed this test. In addition, they had to be roomy enough so that Shirley could wear them for as long as possible before passing them down to me. We would sit there watching the familiar drama between Mama and the increasingly frustrated clerk play out.

Proverbs and sayings kept us in check. We were often reminded that, 'Every day bucket go a well, one day the bucket bottom a go drop out.' Or, 'Every dog have him day, and every puss him 4 o'clock.' 'Chicken merry, hawk deh near' would remind us never to be excited, for something bad was sure to happen. 'Every disappointment is for a good' was supposed to be a consolation. To reinforce the latter, and to help 'build character', Mama would sometimes get us all dressed up for some function, only to tell us, just before we were scheduled to leave, that we weren't going after all.

One of the ways in which my mother punished us was to warn us that if we did not behave and did not study hard, there were certain Houses where we could end up — the Alms House, the Poor House, the Work House or the Court House. They figured prominently in my mother's constant refrains. These were awful places, fit only for beggars, she told us. Telling lies, which always led to envy and stealing, would land us in the Court House and possibly the Work House. This future applied not only to us but to her. If we didn't make it in the world, neither would she. What was it about these Houses where we could end up, depending on the way we lived our lives? It was never clear to me, but the prospect was frightening and the threats made us behave. We had to be grateful to God for what we had; we had to be thrifty and waste nothing; we had to protect our clothes and shoes — in short, we had to be perfect children.

We were also reminded that Mama was making enormous sacrifices to keep us out of these threatening Houses. For example, she only allowed herself one 'draws' — one pair of underwear — in order to save money. For years I imagined that my mother wore the same pair of 'draws' all the time, taking them off only to wash them. Whenever we didn't do well at school, she would say, 'Yu tink I am wearing one draws for nothing?' I felt sorry for her that she had only one pair of 'draws' and wished I could be a brilliant student like Shirley to reassure her that what she was doing was not in vain. I vowed that when I grew up, I would buy her as many 'draws' as she desired.

My father, dark in complexion by comparison with Mama, was the third son in a family of six children. Eric Hugh Anderson was born in Cuba, at the turn of the twentieth century, where his father, Kaiser, had gone to work on the sugar plantations. Kaiser returned to Jamaica years later as one of the leading auctioneers in Kingston. The three boys were the product of the same mother, but my grandmother died when my father was only a baby. After my grandmother's death, my grandfather lost interest in his sons and left them with an aunt, Cordelia, in the small rural town of Balaclava. Cordelia did her best to take care of them, but my grandfather made no provision for anything further than a primary education. Later, Kaiser would marry again. Matilda, his second wife, was an austere, controlling, no-nonsense but well-meaning woman — not unlike my mother — and they never got along. Aunt Matty insisted the boys be brought to Kingston to live with her and learn a skill.

My father was a man of ideas. He loved to read and to write, and he wanted to be a lawyer, a dream which, like my mother, was never achieved. He was sent to learn mechanics, an act of constructive assistance without which he would never have had the opportunity to be a manager in the railway. When Aunt Matty had her own daughter, Ida, she made sure that she had the secondary education that my father and his brothers, too old by then, had been denied.

My earliest memory of my grandfather, Kaiser, is of his occasional visits. He was tall and strapping. I remember him warning me against the dangers of having anyone kiss me, even on my cheeks, in case of germs. Life with him could not have been easy for Matty. Her young cousin Victoria lived with them for a while. With her usual thoughtfulness, Matilda taught her how to sew. But during this time Victoria became pregnant by Kaiser and gave birth to a daughter, Barbara. The beautiful Victoria was made to leave the house, but what always intrigued me about the story was that Matty refused to end her marriage, and despite the obvious strain, dutifully continued to pack a lunch tray for Kaiser every day and arrange for its delivery to his office.

Kaiser eventually became a real estate agent and operated his own business in downtown Kingston, on Beeston Street. But although there was talk of his having owned several properties in Kingston and residential St Andrew, he died penniless, leaving only the marital home on Westminster Road to his widow and daughter, Ida, who became a secretary in a major soft drink firm in Kingston, and eventually married a civil servant and gave birth to my cousin Pamela. In an unexpected twist to this story, Matty eventually took in Victoria's daughter, Barbara, to live with her in the Westminster Road home.

When I was a child, we lived in sections of rented houses mainly in East Kingston, Rollington Town and Franklin Town. These were lower middle-class areas with stinking open drains, and yet the smells I remember are of mangoes rather than sewage, and, inevitably, my mother's abiding Jeyes Fluid and Dettol. Every house had its fruit trees in the yard. I can still hear the sounds of the street vendors calling out their wares — hominy corn and booby egg — and of the local peanut vendor, who was also a ventriloquist, pushing his whistling cart.

The family was always moving house, movements which depended on whether my father had been demoted, promoted or transferred by the railway company. There were times when he was transferred, often with little notice, to rural Jamaica, and this would mean the rest of the family having to rent rooms in Kingston so that our school life would not be disrupted. Daddy would live in housing provided for him above the railway station, which meant that he would lose his small housing allowance, making life even more difficult for us and particularly challenging for my mother, who was the family's money manager.

But, first of all, she had to have money to manage. Depending on the greediness or neediness of the particular 'sweetheart' — the outside woman — my father had at the time, smaller and smaller amounts of money would find their way home. The money my mother would get to manage also depended on the frequency of my father's visits to the rum bar, particularly on the nights he received his pay. When I was about ten years old, the situation got so bad that on one occasion my mother went to the railway pay clerk without my father's knowledge, to demand his pay. The pay clerk told her that he could only hand pay over to people who worked for the railway. Mama retorted that she was my father's wife, that she had children to feed, and above everything else, if he did not give the money to her, she would behave *very* badly. In the end, the pay clerk relented and gave her the salary. When Daddy came home that night, he was, of course, extremely upset. I don't think we had ever seen him so angry. But Mama stood her ground and gave him only pocket money.

The issue of his pay and how it was allocated among his family, his sweethearts and his alcohol was a recurrent theme in the household. He loved my mother. He was prepared to make some sacrifices for his family. But he had to have his nightly visits to the bar, he had to have his Church, he had to have his political meetings, and he had to have his women. He never, ever participated in household chores. I was always amazed at how resilient and quietly defiant he was in the face of my formidable mother. I remember once in Rollington Town when he was ready to go to work, she told him to use the side gate and not the front gate as she had just tidied up that area. My usually obedient father got agitated and said in a loud and decisive voice, 'Side gate, hell!' — and proceeded to use the front gate. My mother just stood and stared at him as he left. Their battles were often childish. Sometimes, to get back at him, instead of preparing and leaving out his dinner, she would cover empty plates and set them on the table as if they contained food. This would lead to another uproar.

We were forced to move so often — sometimes because we couldn't afford the rent, at others because the landlord would decide he didn't want children living in the apartment. On some Sunday mornings my mother and I would get up early, before anyone else was awake, and search through the 'Apartments for Rent' section of the *Gleaner* newspaper. At that time 'apartment' meant a section of a house with a bathroom shared with other tenants. We would also walk from street to street in our neighbourhood looking for signs that read APARTMENTS TO LET — APPLY WITHIN. I am not sure why I was the one chosen to accompany my mother, but this was one of the things we did together that made me feel proud and grown-up. Yet, I always dreaded the work involved in moving, and the uncertainty of going to a new neighbourhood, particularly if it was far from our school. To this day, I feel compelled, when I wake, to read the Classified Ads when there is no longer any need to do so.

Looking back on my mother's life, the most extraordinary thing about her was her determination to be financially independent. She always told us that, in addition to marrying a man who could support us, we girls should eventually own a house in our own name. We were told to avoid 'boy boys'— those who were black, underprivileged, spoke Jamaican patois, and were going nowhere, the kind who would get us pregnant. When I think of it now, she was always setting the example, saving money from the limited means of my father's pay cheque. Despite being dependent on my father economically, she was determined to use those savings to buy her own house and have a title unencumbered by a mortgage. Savings she told us, was to be kept hidden from a husband at all costs.

When I was about ten years old we were surprised to be told that we had another brother, Tony. Later my father informed us that he had had this son before he met my mother but hadn't known how to tell her then about the boy. When Tony's mother migrated to the United States, my father was forced to take him in, and he brought Tony to our home. At that time we lived in Linstead, above the railway station. At first my mother was upset and I can remember the tension in the household and the quarrels between my parents. Eventually, Tony settled in, but this did not last long. His mother, who by then was in the United States, sent for him, and suddenly he wasn't with us any more. My mother, who had developed a relationship with Tony, was both relieved and saddened at his leaving.

And then there was Roy, my aunt Myrtle's son, who came to live with us for a while. For a while Roy brought such joy into our lives. By the time Roy came to live with us he was a handsome 12-year-old and my mother adored him — right colour of brown, 'good hair', and the kind of looks she approved of — that is to say, he was good-looking by Caucasian standards. As girls this was our first experience of having a young man in the house. He was allowed to play outside in the yard in a way that we weren't. And we had to close the bathroom door behind us, because he was 'different' from us. I watched and envied my mother's relationship with him: it seemed he could do no wrong. Roy played cricket constantly and one day the ball nearly knocked his eye out. I remember vividly the fear, the blood, the pain, and my mother playing the doctor role she loved so well. She managed to correct the damage and the doctor who later saw him was astonished that she had handled it so well.

My mother came from a near-white middle-class family on her father's side. They were Jews out of Scotland, the Pearsons. My grandfather was a big drinker and had an awful temper. Nobody messed with him — or they did so at their own risk. At the turn of the century, he made 'buggies', horse-drawn carriages for the wealthy. Most of his family lived in Panama, having gone there like other Jamaicans, to work on the Panama Canal. Many of my cousins arrived from Panama, and their use of Spanish brought a new and exotic flavour to the family. My grandfather built two homes on the property. The larger home housed the main family: my grandfather, my grandmother and my mother. My mother's brother, Uncle Massa, a barber, and her sister Myrtle also lived on the property. My two great-aunts,

Edith and Dell, lived in the smaller house. After my grandfather died in the 1940s, my grandmother struggled to do the best she could, but the property grew run-down. The family yard at 7 Crooks Street is still there, although much of the house, along with the two-room apartment where the aunts lived, has been neglected or destroyed. It was taken over by squatters after Great-aunt Edith died.

The family home in Jones Town, a middle-class area at the time, was well kept by my grandmother. She planted her own vegetables and reared ducks and chickens. She had beautiful antique mahogany furniture, family photographs, and china and silver. It was clear that this was no ordinary home. My grandfather never married my grandmother, though I became aware of this only when she died in the late 1960s and I was asked to place a death announcement on radio. I found out then that her name was Delcina Hall. This meant that my mother, like her siblings, was illegitimate. In those days illegitimacy was a stigma, so I was not surprised that this had been kept a secret.

My Aunt Myrtle washed bottles at a soda bottling plant, Desnoes & Geddes, all her working life. This was menial, repetitive work at minimum wage. We would sometimes visit her on the job and watch her as she hand-washed bottle after bottle. She never complained. She eventually met her husband, who was doing the same type of work, and they had a happy marriage.

Unfortunately, my mother had a strange relationship with her family. Until I was about ten years old, every Sunday afternoon we would visit my grandmother and Aunt Edith —

by then my grandfather had died. Then suddenly we stopped going. My mother never told us why.

The ritual, while it lasted, was fun. We would come home from Sunday school at Galilee Gospel Hall, a branch of the Brethren Church, to the smell of dinner in the early afternoon: my mother's rice and peas served with either roast beef and roasted potatoes or chicken. In addition, there would be salad — sliced tomatoes and cucumber — and potato pudding done the old-fashioned way, cooked in a traditional iron Dutch pot with hot coals on top and underneath. Coconut was added to the pudding to make the top wet and sugary. These were the special Sunday kitchen smells.

After dinner, we would take a bus from Rollington Town across town to visit Grandma in Jones Town. My memories of Jones Town include the neighbourhood's open drains and ensuring that we never walked in them, but skipped over them. I remember getting off the bus and having to walk a little distance to my grandmother's house, me holding my mother's hand firmly while my younger sister Roma held on to me, and my older sister Shirley holding my mother's other hand. Letting go of my mother's hand meant a spanking right there in the street, so we clung for dear life.

My grandmother's home was full of exciting things. She raised chickens and ducks. We were fascinated by the ducks. The strange smell of duck shit permeated the entire yard. In spite of this we loved to watch the way the ducks waddled and listen to them quack. They brought our early schoolbooks alive. Also in my grandmother's house were wonderful photographs of my mother when she was younger, and of her wedding. She had been beautiful. At that age I could not quite equate the stunning beauty queen in the pictures with my mother, who although still physically beautiful, had by now grown ugly in personality.

But what I liked most about being in my grandmother's house was her corn meal porridge. She always served me in what I regarded as 'my' yellow enamel cup, which matched the colour of the corn meal. She was an excellent cook and had passed on these skills to my mother.

I also associate my grandmother's house with my male cousin Jackie. Jackie was the child of my grandmother's niece, Mrs Estick, but had been brought up by my grandmother. My mother adored him and treated him as her own son. One day, while visiting my grandmother, we realised that Jackie was seriously ill; the grown-ups were talking in whispers, saying that the doctors did not know what was wrong with Jackie and that, despite medical treatment, he was not getting any better. There was talk about something called *obeah*. A huge, deep sore was visible on his leg, which grew thinner and thinner, and out of proportion to the other leg. We thought he was dying, but my mother was confident that she could heal him. She took over his care and before long he was well again, although the bad leg never regained its former size.

Sunday afternoons at Grandma's were some of the few pleasurable memories for me growing up. I remember her as warm, loving and quiet — totally unlike my mother. After Mama mysteriously stopped these visits, it was 17 years before I saw my grandmother again. I remember visiting her in the hospital. The tiny woman in the bed in the dark hospital room bore little or no resemblance to my grandmother. Her curly greying hair, once long enough so that she could sit on it and usually done in plaits, was spread out on the pillows. She just lay there without speaking, her eyes closed. I remember thinking that people change when they are about to die. My mother told us she was dying and that dying was part of life and something that we had to accept. We had to be strong. No tears — that was for weak people. My grief was made easier because, as far as I was concerned, the woman in the bed was not my grandmother. That was my first experience of death.

By the time I was seven or eight I had lost my baby fat and become thin as well as tall. I was always the tallest in my class and felt strange and awkward. I had huge eyes and thought I was ugly. I was also the darkest in my family and my mother often compared me with my father, who by then had fulfilled all the prophecy of my grandparents and turned out to be good for nothing, as all blacks were — at least that was how my mother put it. Because my colour was unacceptable, like my father's, my destiny too was to be good for nothing. My mother told me this constantly, and I soon developed a defence mechanism. I withdrew into myself, became very quiet, and struggled constantly to prove that I was as good as my sisters, regardless of what Mama said. This withdrawal would suddenly erupt into something quite different whenever my mother accused me of something I felt as unjust. My colour was God-given and I may have been part of a race that was unacceptable, but some things — such as my sisters relaxing while I was made to do housework — I railed at having to put up with it. My 'brown' sisters were not allowed to help. I was resentful, yet there was a sense in which I accepted this was the role of the darkest one in the family. Until I was in my fifties I thought of myself as very dark because in my family I was always called 'black'.

During those days there were few refrigerators in homes and the ice company would deliver to individual houses. We used to take 25 pounds of ice, and I was the one who had to haul it from the truck to the icebox in the kitchen. On one of those mornings I dropped the ice on my toe. I can still feel the pain. I screamed, then quickly shut up, picked up the ice and took it into the house. Only after I had placed it in the icebox did I run away to cry. I just could not deal with another flogging. My toe hurt for days, and when I put on my shoes the pain got worse, but I bore it quietly, the way I knew my mother would have wanted me to.

My sisters and I always shared a double bed. We enjoyed sleeping close together, and it provided comfort, particularly when my father returned home drunk at night and our mother started cursing. In spite of her response to his drinking and philandering, he never stopped. We girls would huddle close together, hoping that things wouldn't get violent. We also hated it when we heard our mother cry. This was a heart-rending sound like a dog howling. We couldn't handle hearing this from our Mama, a woman who seemed so strong.

One night she attacked my father physically and when he hit her back, she slipped and fell. We lived above the railway station in Old Harbour then. I was 12 years old. We were in bed, as usual, when Daddy came home drunk. She cursed him about the usual things — his drinking and his current sweethearts. She was concerned about one in particular, who was the latest postmistress to arrive in town. Mama knew her by name. We heard her scream as her body hit the floor. Because we were always expecting something horrible to happen to one or both of them as a result of their quarrels, our darkest fears had now been realised. Daddy had hurt Mama physically.

We ran out of our bedroom to help her. I can hardly remember what happened after that, but suddenly everyone was helping her up off the floor and we were all frightened. Later we would learn that she had sprained her back. She had to wear bandages around her torso and therefore also around her small child-feeding breasts and down the length of her body to just short of her abdomen. The adhesive bandages stuck to her, and she had to use Johnson's baby powder to soothe the inevitable itching and discomfort. But she still had her housework to do and carried on. The sprain was just one more cross to bear. Things would be so much easier for the entire family, I thought, if Daddy would just stop drinking, stop philandering and come home to us at night.

In many ways my father was a mystery to me. During the week he worked long days and many nights. In between, he would frequent the rum bar, which was always close by, and visit his sweetheart of the moment. My father was also involved in an organisation called 'The Lodge' — the Masonic Lodge. My mother teased him about it, trying to find out more about this secret group, but she never got answers to her probing questions, such as 'Did they brand you like a cow when you became a member?'

On Sunday, however, everything changed. My father was a lay preacher in the Anglican Church and he took his duties seriously. Whenever he preached or participated from the altar of the church, even his accent changed to one that sounded British and authoritarian. He became the father we did not know when he was preaching from the pulpit. Everyone said that he had a way with words. He was a good communicator and a powerful preacher. His tones were mellow and he knew how to colour his words. I often wonder if my communication skills and my voice came from him.

By Friday, my mother would have his 'priestly' robes clean and ready for Sunday. These were long gowns, white over black, and had to be impeccable. In the meantime, he would do the research for his sermon and then sit at an old typewriter, pecking away with one finger. During this preparatory period he would sometimes spend a great deal of time in the bathroom where it was peaceful and quiet. My mother would keep telling him to hurry up. He would reply in his finest British accent, 'Don't bother me now, Esmine. Don't you understand I am doing my ablutions!' I always wondered what he was doing, locked up for so long in the bathroom. Did he do something different from what we did in the bathroom? Was this something to do with being a man? When Sunday morning arrived he would dress up in his robes, Bible in hand, and assume the aura of a holy man.

It was important to Daddy that we observe him in church. Wherever we lived, he would be involved in lay preaching. In our earlier years while we lived in East Kingston, he was with St George's Anglican Church in downtown Kingston, which was run by Canon R.O.C. King. Then there was the church in Old Harbour that we attended with him although we were members of the Brethren Church. Later on, in Spanish Town, the Anglican Cathedral was under the leadership of Canon B.C. Jones. We children would go whenever our father was preaching. Our mother never went, although she approved of our going. Her job was to ensure that, just like Daddy, we were well turned out for church in our Sunday best. Daddy would seat us in the front row and then go to the vestry to put on his 'vestments' and get ready for the procession into the church with the rector and other clergy.

Soon however, Roma and I were given to giggling so much that we were moved to the back. We laughed at everything. In church, everything seemed funny. No matter how our parents admonished us, we couldn't help ourselves. Finally, Daddy had what he thought was a brilliant idea. He decided to make us sit in separate areas. But Roma would look around to see where he had positioned me and I would do the same, and the minute we saw something that amused us both, we would be eyeing each other and laughing again. Over the years the giggling never stopped.

But the rest of the time, Daddy lived his life the way he wanted to, and women and alcohol were very much a part of that. I don't think my mother cared for sex. She always described it as nasty, and said that when women did it often, they were loose and careless. In any case, she said, it would wear your body down. Men like my father who had sex with other women were careless and no good, she said, and caught sexual diseases on their penises. She was, from time to time, engaged in some secret ritual with my father where the Dettol and some type of ointment came into play. Often the rooms we lived in had little privacy, and I remember once, when I was about six years old, peeping into their room. They were sitting on the bed, facing each other. My mother had my father's limp penis in her hand. There was a bowl of water on the bedside table. She dipped the cotton wool in the Dettol solution, cleaned his penis and then applied ointment. I stood there transfixed. It was the first time I had seen a penis and I wondered why my father had that 'thing' in front of him that needed that type of care; something that I didn't have. My mother cursed him throughout the ritual: *'no good'; 'you can't do without me'; 'you are bringing diseases home to me and I won't allow you to have sex with me and give me these diseases'; 'you are slack'* and *'if you don't stop seeing that woman, I will kill you.'*

My father just sat there looking hopeless and helpless. I never told anyone what I had seen. I felt that if I did, I would be punished terribly. And, in any case, my sisters wouldn't believe me if I told them of this 'thing' Daddy had in front of him. The next time I saw him I wondered where he had put his 'thing', as it was not visible through his pants. I wondered whether it would need that special care from my mother forever or whether it was like our cuts and bruises that she cared for from time to time. The whole experience made me feel sick, and very ashamed of myself for having watched.

No matter what was happening in the household, though, my sisters and I loved one another and got along quite well. Shirley, the eldest, was bright and pretty, and a little detached from and superior to us. She grew up differently from us, although we were in the same family. My parents made it known from the start that Shirley, as the firstborn, was the queen, and we accepted this. My sister Roma and I were closer. Roma was lucky because she was the 'wash belly', the last baby to come out of my mother's belly, until my brother Maurice was born years later. My parents felt that we needed to take care of her. I still feel that way. Shirley did not suffer fools gladly and kept to herself. I never blamed her for thinking Roma and I were silly. She just couldn't stand our giggling and our need, at six or seven years old, to play 'dolly house' under the mango tree when we lived in East Kingston on Jackson Road. We loved playing shop too, taking turns as customer and shopkeeper. We would use dirt to represent sugar and flour, place it in small packages of paper and imitate the shop owners in our neighbourhood. Those were good times. In our play world, we were kind and loving mummies, but also strict. Our dolls, our 'children', lived in a world far different from ours, a world in which it was all right to enjoy themselves and where the saying 'Chicken merry, hawk deh near' had no relevance.

The one thing I did that would create a lasting bond with my father was to accompany him to political meetings. I suppose you might say I was a born PNP. Both my parents supported the People's National Party (PNP) and it never occurred to either of them to consider the Jamaica Labour Party (JLP). My father was a stronger supporter than my mother. Though she always voted PNP, Mama never understood why people got involved in organisations of any kind. As a young girl, she had been an ardent member of the Roman Catholic Church, but when she asked her priests questions, their answers were never satisfactory.

So she left that church, never to return. In any case, she would tell us, now she had four children and that took up all her time.

However strange it is when I think of it now, politics and the Manleys were a presence in my life even then. As I grew up, my father would tell me about this great party, the PNP, and about its extraordinary leader and founder — Norman Washington Manley. He explained that Mr Manley could be anything he wanted to be and could live anywhere he wanted to, given his awesome talents, particularly as a lawyer, but that he had chosen to remain in Jamaica and enter politics. Then I heard about the stalwarts like Florizel Augustus Glasspole, known as the 'Brown Bomber', William 'Commodore' Seivright, Wills O. Isaacs, and O.T. Fairclough, the first general secretary of the party. These were names I got to know by heart. The left-wing group, my father told me, was led by Richard Hart, and included Ken Hill and Arthur Henry, and there seemed to be some big confusion between the two wings of the party. My father talked about the PNP a great deal, as it represented hard work, excellence and competence, virtues he wanted his children to possess.

On the other hand, the JLP, founded by Alexander Bustamante, Norman Manley's first cousin, was the opposite of the PNP in that Bustamante was not a 'man of letters', as my father put it. Though closely related, the two men had little to do with each other. Unlike Manley, a well-respected Rhodes Scholar and Oxford graduate, Bustamante's dealings, I was constantly reminded, were suspect. My father told many unbelievable stories about Bustamante's life — that he was a Spanish grandee and a moneylender. Daddy said he was not a man who discussed ideas. Like Manley, my father was in love with ideas. These two parties divided Jamaica into members of the PNP called 'Comrades' and members of the JLP called 'Labourites'. Growing up, I always knew I had to be a comrade. My father made it clear that educated people went into the PNP.

My indoctrination into politics began before I was ten years old, when I attended public meetings with Daddy just up the road from where we lived in East Kingston. There were famous public meeting spots all over Jamaica, and in the East Kingston constituency one such spot was at the corner of Jackson Road — the road we lived on — and Giltress Sreet. The preparation for a public meeting began at least one week before the actual date, when cars with loudspeakers attached to the roof drove through the area where the meeting was to be held. There were at least two men in each car, one holding the bullhorn. I never saw a woman doing this; it was a role for men. There was an air of great anticipation surrounding these announcements. My sisters and I would run to the gate to get a taste of all the excitement. The loudspeaker would bellow: *'Tonight, tonight, come and hear the stalwarts of the People's National Party — the Brown Bomber, Florizel Augustus Glasspole, Wills Ogilvie Isaacs, William Seivwright, and the leader of the party, Norman Washington Manley. Don't miss it!'* This was accompanied by the blaring of the popular PNP songs of the day. The car or van would roam the area repeating the announcements. When the meeting day arrived, I knew that I would be there at my father's side, listening to speeches whose words I could not understand but whose message I somehow knew was important.

On that day there would be further activity: banners had to be put up as a backdrop to the platform, lights installed, and of course a high platform built so that the crowd could see the speakers. By the time things got underway there were always many people seated in an orderly fashion on the platform. My father would lift me onto his shoulders and I would crane my neck to see, as my father pointed speakers out and I put faces to the many names he had so often mentioned. These men could talk — even at that age I understood that. My father was right. These were men of ideas.

By the time I was ten, in 1951, the PNP had already lost the two elections since universal adult suffrage had been granted seven years earlier. Manley had even lost his seat in the 1944 elections, but, great man that he was, my father told me, he remained as PNP leader, building the party.

Bustamante's message of 'a little more bread and a little more butter' in the 1940s made far more sense to the majority of people than Manley's vision of education for all and political independence. My father felt that this was only to be expected, as the majority of people could not read. I would often hear him from our rooms above the railway station as he had arguments at work throughout the day with travellers on the platform. He talked like the PNP leaders, sharing his ideas. For all his interest in the political process, however, my father never considered going into representational politics; he felt this would be held against him and would jeopardise his job. Representational politics was for other people, not for him. In any case, his boss, the man who headed the railway, Mr Hamilton, was perceived to be a Labourite. In spite of his caution, my mother felt that my father was discriminated against for being a member of the PNP. This was evident from the inconsiderate way in which he was transferred from railway station to railway station across Jamaica, often with little notice. One of the things I learned early was that when your political affiliation was known, it could be used against you.

Meeting night was one of the few evenings my father chose to come home instead of stopping at the bar. He would remind me that morning that he would be returning home to take me with him. We would arrive early, when music was playing; people were dancing and some of the lesser-knowns in the party would be at the mike making the earlier speeches. The big guns arrived later, Norman Manley arriving last. The atmosphere was festive, the crowds large. People pushed against each other jovially. It was like a gigantic family gathering — comrades meeting and enjoying one another and showing off to the Labourites.

For me it was like attending a concert. There was excitement in the air. Speaker after speaker denigrated the JLP and Bustamante. When it was time for our member of parliament, Florizel Augustus Glasspole, to speak, the atmosphere rose to fever pitch. The chairman had a special role to play, not only to keep the meeting interesting but also to announce each speaker. The chairman announced him: 'And now, a man who had his origins in the trade union movement, a man who won in his seat in both elections, the leader of the House for the PNP, a vice-president of the PNP, a man in whom we are all pleased, ladies and gentlemen, I give you the member of parliament for the constituency of East Kingston, the Brown Bomber' — by this time his voice had reached a crescendo —

'Florizel Augustus Glasspole'. The crowd would give their MP the biggest cheering ever.

The Brown Bomber ran to the microphone shadow-boxing, then stood still, listening to the cheers of the audience. Finally, raising both hands, he gestured to them to cool down. Then we heard his voice for the first time, as the crowd grew silent. As my mother would say, 'If you dropped a pin, you would hear it.' This was the moment. His voice boomed out over the microphone, 'Comrade Chairman ...' and the crowd went wild again. Speaker after speaker was announced in this way.

The final spot was left for Manley, the major presentation of the night. Norman Washington Manley was a handsome, copper-coloured man with aquiline features. That is how my father described him. He often wore three-piece suits with a rosebud in his lapel, but for public meetings he was casually dressed in a long-sleeved coloured shirt. A proper man, as Daddy used to say; man to look up to. The announcement for him lasted longer than anyone else's. He was the leader and founder of the party. He was the eminent lawyer who had won case after case. Stories about him in court were legendary. He was the man who would lead Jamaica into independence. When he rose to speak, everyone in the audience went crazy. My father, who worked long hours for the railway, was often exhausted, and sometimes slept through other speeches, but when Norman Manley spoke, he was wide awake. He didn't want to miss a word coming out of the mouth of this great man.

Having been properly introduced, Manley rose and walked purposefully to the microphone, appearing confident, yet somewhat shy. He stood there with his arms clasped at his side, his stomach pushed slightly forward and a half-smile on his face. Clearly he was pleased with the crowd's reaction: enthusiasm bordering on worship. That was the norm with this constituency of East Kingston, a solid PNP stronghold.

Even as a child I was fascinated by the way Norman Manley spoke. His words were slightly, ever so slightly, muffled, uttered in a singsong way and as if he had cotton in his mouth, and a whole generation of Jamaicans would try to talk just like him. We never quite accomplished it. His control of the English language was amazing and he used it to full effect. Though not given to drama, he was a powerful speaker and a man of enormous presence.

Such evenings were pure theatre. The backdrop, the stage, the props, the audience, and the speakers with their different roles to play. Each was at once reflective, serious and happy — keeping the audience engaged. I loved attending those meetings with my father. They were some of the few occasions when he chose to let me be with him and my mother approved. They were a highlight of my life.

The PNP talked a lot about Jamaicans governing themselves — 'a modicum of self-government' was the way they put it. My father tried to explain to me why the PNP was never called 'Labour' even though the party was modelled after the Labour Party in England. I remember him saying that it had something to do with the fact that the PNP did not come out of a trade union movement — Bustamante had already taken control of that area. But, he said, the fact that the PNP did not have the word 'Labour' in its name did not mean that it wasn't for the masses who were labourers. I didn't quite understand this then, but I did know that the PNP had a great tradition and that it was a party we could be proud of. As for England, for me it was just a cold place far away where many poor Jamaicans went in order to better themselves.

My father's job at the railway kept him working morning, noon and night, and although he wasn't at the launch of the party on September 18, 1938, he read about it in detail in the *Gleaner*. Sir Stafford Cripps, a member of the British Labour Party, who was holidaying in Jamaica at the time, was the guest speaker. It was held at the Ward Theatre in downtown Kingston and was a grand affair. The PNP was the only mass political party in Jamaica at the time and Bustamante was on the platform, although he was not asked to speak. At the time he headed the Bustamante Industrial Trade Union (BITU).

Daddy used to tell the story of how these two first cousins had started out together within the same movement and then something happened, he wasn't quite sure what it was, that made Bustamante form his own party in 1943, just in time for the first general elections under universal adult suffrage. What my father did know was that, whatever happened, it was Bustamante's fault. He could not be trusted. When Bustamante was imprisoned for his fiery speeches, Manley and members of the PNP left wing had built the BITU and kept it alive. After Bustamante came out of prison, however, he abandoned the PNP, accused them of wanting to take over his union, and went on to form his own party. Daddy used all this to emphasise the kind of person Bustamante was. The break was the beginning of two equally large parties in Jamaica fighting for power every five years, and supported by members who bordered on the fanatic, like Daddy.

Election time was thrilling. The first election that I remember vividly was in 1955, the third election under adult suffrage. Both my parents voted. Here was an opportunity for the PNP to win for the first time with Norman Manley installed as Chief Minister. It would now be possible for the party to promote its ideas of independence. I remember well that the slogan that caught the attention of the people was 'Sweep them out'. At meetings comrades used brooms to demonstrate how the JLP would be swept out. I attended more meetings than ever with my father around that time. We stayed off the roads when the JLP was meeting, just in case there was stone-throwing or other kind of hostility. Norman Manley took to the hustings. Bustamante took to the hustings. I remember visiting Parliament one day when I was in school and seeing Bustamante in person for the first time. I was awed by his appearance — very tall and lanky in a three-piece suit and with a flash of beautiful, greying hair. I thought his presence was impressive, but I couldn't tell my father that. I was overwhelmed, and understood for the first time why the masses adored him.

The PNP did indeed sweep those elections, and our member of parliament, the Brown Bomber, became the minister of education. East Kingston was proud, and Daddy and I attended the 'thank you' meetings. Now that the party was in power, my father emphasised to us that party members should never ask it for anything. We were there to serve the party, and it was there to serve the country overall, not individual comrades.

Chapter 2

Things were hard for my family when I was growing up, but I didn't realise this until I was much older. My mother always felt that what my father did was slave labour and that he was grossly underpaid. She blamed all this on the CEO of the railway, Mr Ted Hamilton, whose name she pronounced as 'Hambleton'. We grew up hearing this name spoken in the most disparaging manner. Mama would exhort Daddy to go and speak to Mr 'Hambleton' about making things better — he needed to know, she said, how disruptive it was for the family when Daddy was transferred and how this often meant less money to spend when sometimes we were forced to keep two homes. Would Daddy agree to see Mr 'Hambleton' or did he want her to go? 'Sweethearts' and 'Hambleton' were two of the villains of my early childhood.

But life was just the way it was, and we were not allowed to complain, not allowed to envy each other or anyone else. One of my most memorable church dresses was made of a material with flowers in shades of green. I called it my 'callaloo' dress because I hated callaloo, a green leafy vegetable similar to spinach that was stewed down with saltfish, a Jamaican staple. My mother would use a spoon to force it down my throat. I can still feel the cold hardness of the spoon inside my mouth as she pressed it on my tongue, almost choking me, all the while reminding me how good callaloo was for me. *It is for your own good.* How I hated those words! Why did everything that was good for me have to be associated with terrible experiences?

I was forced to wear the callaloo dress one day to a school function. I begged Mama not to make me wear it as it was ugly and I didn't want the children laughing at me. She insisted. I walked to school, holding a red umbrella to protect me from the rays of the sun. This, of course, only increased the heat. I remember not caring any more how I looked or who saw me — I was just a sad little girl, feeling desolate and ugly on her way to school.

We were part of an upwardly mobile working class, but both parents, and to a greater extent my mother, recognised, with urgency, that it was education that would get us out of that class. Everything in our family life was focused on that. There were many sacrifices to be made by all because bus fares had to be found, books had to be bought, uniforms had to be made, and even though we had only one uniform each, we had to be the best dressed in the school. My mother often told us how impressed our neighbours were with the way she turned us out for school. Some of her finest moments came when she was praised for such efforts.

My father's sacrifice was that he had to stay at the railway with its long, stressful, uncertain hours. He felt that moving from that secure job was too great a risk for someone who had four children and a wife to care for. He needed a steady, reliable income to pay for his children's education. This was fairly typical of families like ours in the 1950s and 1960s, but what distinguished us from the rest was the passionate emphasis that our parents placed on education. It was not just education first, but education instead of going to a fair; education instead of pretty clothes; education instead of gifts at Christmas; education almost instead of life itself. It was my parents' reason for being. So we heard about education ad nauseum.

For our part, we were expected to work to make life easier through education. What this meant for me was few clothes — mostly hand-me-downs, walking at least one bus route to school, little or no fun, and few friends. We were to be our own friends. We needed no one else and, in any case, the wrong kind of 'friends' could put us in danger — danger of being corrupted and led astray. Or we could end up envying them what they had, which would be a major sin. Having fun was also a sin. 'Chicken merry, hawk deh near.' Not until recently have I learned to feel that it is safe to have fun.

Incidents such as the callaloo moments — when my mother would force-feed me the awful vegetable — made me feel like less than a person on the one hand, yet defiant and aggressive on the other. I would swallow it and cry my eyes and heart out, at which stage the strap would reappear. As with the castor oil, my sisters never understood why I didn't just give in and do what Mama wanted us to do. But it was never an option for me, although this attitude meant that I was in an ongoing battle with my mother over even the simplest of things. I constantly defied her authority, needing as I did to have reasons for doing things. My sisters begged me not to fight her so much, and so did my father, but I couldn't help myself. I talked back and fought her every step of the way, and longed for the day when I would reach the age of consent, 21, and could just walk out the door and begin to live. Writing this, I am reliving those unfair days and realising where I got such a strong sense of injustice. This would serve me well later, in the 1970s, when justice emerged as a passion in my life.

By the time I got to Franklin Town Primary School, I was an emotional mess. I was shy and cried easily. I was beginning to grow tall and skinny. I was told that my eyes and lips were too large. None of my sisters had this problem. I was, after all, like my black, no-good father — a message that had been drummed into me.

One of the few ways in which I received positive attention from my family was by mimicking. I liked watching people and imitating them, and I was good at it. I was developing a talent for performance. I received attention from the family when I did my acts and often did them on request. My family couldn't wait for me to come home from school to entertain them, and this made me feel that I had something to give — less like the odd one out. As I write this I feel tearful and am not sure why. I suppose that in playing a part I was hiding my true feelings, that when the 'play' was over, it was back to the real world until I was asked to perform again. I can hear the requests now, even from my mother: 'Beverley, why don't you imitate so and so?' It was like winding up a toy and watching it perform. But it was all that I had. Sometimes I wonder how this affected me later in life — performing so others would like me. It makes me sad but also grateful for this gift, this survival mechanism that got me through some rough times.

Roma and I walked to Franklin Town School together what seemed like a long way. Our uniform was standard — a blue skirt with white blouse, brown shoes and white socks. A blue tie to match the pleated skirt. When we entered the school we were amazed at how different it was from our previous preparatory school. It seemed so big. The headmaster and headmistress were Mr and Mrs Vidal Smith. Mrs Smith was a short woman, large breasted with a small waist, who always combed her perpetually straightened hair neatly and severely back into a bun low on her neck. Her husband was a slight man with a thin face and nose and 'good' hair — based on our Jamaican obsession that qualified hair as superior according to the extent of its Caucasian-ness. I often wondered what the headmaster and his wife were like when they were alone together, this big-breasted woman and this slight man. Of course, these were private thoughts that I could express only to Roma, as I was sure this was not only a slack thing to do but also a sin.

I paid no attention to boys. This was such a major sin that I was not willing to defy my mother. I thought I would die and go to hell if a boy even looked at me — and I was not ready for that.

I had a best friend at Franklin Town School, Yvonne Huie, who lived across the road from school. Her mother behaved strangely from time to time. I don't know how it was for Yvonne. I visited her home occasionally without Mama's knowing. Yvonne was brown and pretty, with dimples. I also had deep dimples. We would eat lunch and gossip together.

School began with devotions, which were taken seriously and everyone had to be at school on time for them. The Smiths were excellent educators and ran the school in a disciplined way. I have often maintained had I left school after Franklin Town and never gone to another school, I would have had an education second to none. We would line up form by form in the large schoolyard and stand still until we heard the sound of Beethoven's Fifth permeating the air. It was a wonderful and uplifting sound and I looked forward to the feeling I experienced each morning as I listened to it. It made me forget home and what home was like. It made me know that there was another world where people wrote that type of music so that others could listen. Devotion was a special time of day for me.

My form teacher was Miss Jennings, who at the time must have been in her early twenties. She was brown-skinned with short, straightened hair and she taught us all subjects. She was an excellent teacher and chose me as one of her favourite students. Something in me apparently touched her.

Miss Jennings was a loving, caring woman who did everything to assuage my deepest fears and to help me out of my shyness. She recognised early that I had a talent for the theatre and encouraged me to develop it, so that soon I was entering and winning elocution contests for the school. It was as if there were two different people operating within the same body. It became easier for me to be one, knowing that the other was there somewhere. This paradox, this tension between the powerful and the powerless within me, haunts me to this day.

Although Miss Jennings was strict, as long as you did your work, everything was fine. She never spanked me, and if she spanked anyone at all it was rare. She was an anomaly in Jamaican schools where it was felt that the only effective discipline was corporal punishment.

I shared with Miss Jennings stories about my home life. She was interested in me and I loved that. Then one day when I was about 11 years old, she told me that she was going to her brother's home in Buff Bay and she wanted to take me with her for a two-week vacation. I explained to her that this would be impossible, as my mother almost never allowed us out of her sight to go anywhere and certainly not with a stranger. When she insisted, I told her to go and talk with my mother. I was anxious about this meeting because Mama might think that I was using Miss Jennings to put pressure on her, but I took the risk because I really wanted to go. I worried myself sick. Thank God my mother liked her, and once my mother liked you, once her 'spirit took to you', everything was fine. She prided herself on being psychic — having 'goat mouth', as she put it. She gave Miss Jennings a long list of warnings, but eventually agreed to let me go. I think that was the happiest day of my life, though I had to contain those feelings because 'Every disappointment is for a good' and '<u>Chicken merry, hawk deh near</u>'. My mother could easily back out of her decision for a 'good' reason.

This time, thankfully, she did not. At the beginning of the summer holidays, my mother prepared me well, ensuring that I had enough underwear to wash every day and hang in the sun to prevent germs, and enough clothes so that she would not be embarrassed. I was told to mind my manners so that everyone would know that I came from a good home. But most of all, I was warned that any kind of misbehaviour would be dealt with swiftly and firmly. I am still not sure why my mother allowed me to go. I think she may have felt that having a teacher love me was a good thing for my education and therefore my future;

that Miss Jennings was a good role model. Perhaps someday I would be a teacher, I thought, and make Mama's joy complete. Teachers were highly respected by my parents. There was no better way for a woman to serve her country than by teaching, and all her girls would have professions, so that, unlike her, they would never, ever be dependent on a man.

My only memories of the country, of rural Jamaica, were from when I was younger, before primary school, when Daddy had his way and I was sent to Balaclava in St Elizabeth, for a two-week stay with his Great-aunt Cordelia's niece Beryl and her husband Noel. Noel was a farmer and they lived in a little house on their own land. Daddy wanted me to experience the challenges of rural life. I had to fetch water on my head every day from a nearby spring and use a 'pit toilet' for the first time. I didn't enjoy that visit and was glad to return home after one week.

My only other rural experience was in Linstead. My godmother lived there on the main street in this rural town, and when I was about six years old, she took me to stay with her for two weeks. I hated it because she made me sleep on a 'grip' — a large suitcase that she covered with folded blankets to make it less uncomfortable. When my mother came to visit and check on me, and saw where I was sleeping, she cursed my godmother and took me home immediately. I really felt that I was one of her beloved children then. I was so happy to go home. I cannot remember any of my sisters being sent away on holiday.

From the moment Miss Jennings and I left Kingston on the 'country bus', the adventure began. It was at once frightening and exhilarating. The journey to Buff Bay took about three and a half hours, and I did not think we could make it without having an accident. We travelled along the Junction Road, known for its endless curves and signs proclaiming Numerous Curves Ahead. Every seat was taken. Miss Jennings allowed me to have the window seat so that I could see what was happening along the way. On boarding I had observed that the baggage section was the top of the bus. I remembered the need for these from my early childhood, because on the railway there were special baggage trains and baggage cars — it seemed Jamaicans had a lot of baggage. The top of the bus was so loaded that I wondered how it would move and take corners without the baggage falling off. The bus seemed to take the curves on two wheels with the baggage swaying from one side to the other at every turn. The sideman had ensured that it was all securely tied with ropes, but could ropes do the job? I was reminded of the only time I had been on a Ferris wheel, with my father at the annual St George's Fair. The experience was scary and I had vowed never to repeat it.

I recall that Miss Jennings pointed out Castleton Gardens to me and told me how beautiful they were. What seemed like hours later, we arrived in Buff Bay, which was breathtakingly beautiful — like a rain forest. The sight of the sea surprised me, as I hadn't realised that Buff Bay was on the coast and that the cottage we would stay at was by the sea. Miss Jennings's brother worked at the hospital, which entitled him to living quarters there in a cottage with his wife and children.

I went to the beach a lot, something I was never allowed to do at home because of my mother's fear of the water. Being at

Buff Bay also included daily devotions in the home. Miss Jennings's brother would lead these prayers in addition to saying grace at mealtime. Although we were on hospital grounds, this did not intrude on our lives as the grounds were large and the cottages were situated away from the facility itself. The sea, the all-encompassing sea, gave us the feeling that we were separate and apart from everything else. Miss Jennings also took the opportunity to have many conversations with me about life generally and to allow me to experience new things. She became my role model. One day I would be like her. She eventually became headmistress of Franklin Town School.

At Franklin Town, I also participated in sports. I finally grew to just over five feet seven inches, and was always among the tallest in my class. I had long legs and arms. Though I felt awkward, I was good at high jump and sprinting — not exceptional, but I held my own.

After the Smiths retired, they were succeeded by the Hanchards. Things were never quite the same after that, but they kept up the excellent standard of the school. Mr Hanchard was a strict disciplinarian who used the strap often. A boy once told a lie on me and I was sent to the headmaster's office, where I was flogged by Mr Hanchard himself. I remember waiting outside his door for some time, an act of torture that I am sure was part of the punishment. I was finally called in and asked to explain myself. I told the truth. He chose to believe his son, and I was beaten. I recall closing my eyes, vowing not to cry, and receiving several lashes on the palms of my hands. It hurt, but I was determined not to give him the satisfaction of seeing me cry. My experiences with my mother helped — I could feel pain and not give in. Defiance was my defence mechanism.

As part of this defiance, when I was told to return to my classroom, I walked home instead and told my mother what had happened. I took the long way home in a fury, knowing how much my mother hated lies and knowing also that she would believe me and understand that an injustice had been done. She knew that I was not a liar. I prayed that this would turn out to be one of those rare occasions when she would put on her clothes and go to the school to take on the teacher. Instead, my mother listened to me, took a good look at me, and told me to march back to school. She made it clear that at school, the teacher, and particularly the head teacher, was in charge. It was a deeply humiliated little girl who walked slowly back to school. After that I never went near Mr Hanchard again.

During my early years while Daddy preached at St George's Church, we attended Sunday school, at my mother's insistence, at Galilee Gospel Hall in Rollington Town. Part of the Brethren Church system, this was fundamentalist religion at the highest level. But Sunday school was enjoyable; we found it fun. Mr and Mrs Kerr were the lay ministers of the church. Every time Mr Kerr asked for those who wanted to repent and know the Lord, those who wanted to cast away earthly things and rest in the Lord and those who were willing to obey God's will, my sisters and I would raise our hands and approach the altar. In fact, we went for the gifts that children were given as a result of this: animals, mainly fishes cut out of cloth with a felt backing so they could be placed on a felt board. We loved collecting them and showing them to Mama with pride. After all, this was a sure sign that we were continuing to move away from sin. We therefore got 'saved' every Sunday, and everything was back to normal on Monday.

Sunday school was fun too because of the annual picnic. Occasionally different sites were chosen, but mostly it took place at Doncaster, on those grounds on the sea near Rollington Town, and Mama always allowed us to go. We would take our own lunch and the church would provide sugar buns for dessert and 'wash', lemonade made with water, sugar and a little lime. The liquid filled our bellies. There was this unique feeling that came from having sugar buns and 'wash', a feeling that left you sleepy and full, as if you could never feel empty again.

The Anglican Church was completely different, formal and organised, but we loved it also. Daddy liked going to the night service. Roma and I giggled a lot. The best part was that afterwards, Daddy always took us to an ice cream parlour on Windward Road. Ice cream parlours were special, with small, round, white tables, all nice and clean, and filled with the fresh, sweet smell that came from the ice cream itself. The ice cream was always served with plain cake. We ordered what we wanted. This was freedom. We took some home for Mama, who never went to church, although she spoke to God every day. She said she had the capacity to bring God down into her bed and talk to him face to face.

My mother never allowed us to see her naked, and so it was with great interest that, while we lived above the Old Harbour railway station, Roma and I discovered one of our windows looked down into the women's toilet. The market higglers would sometimes stay in the station to catch the early train to Kingston and use the toilets as an area to wash themselves. The higglers brought a new energy to the railway office downstairs. There was a great deal of talking and quarrelling as they discussed the issues of the day, such as drought, or too much rain and flooding, or which foods were scarce or not. They took over the station as their own and my father had no problem with this. Roma and I loved spying on them from our vantage point upstairs. But we couldn't let Mama catch us at it.

We watched in fascination as the higglers stripped down, the women baring their large breasts and cleaning their private parts. Observing these bodies and giggling, my sister and I felt a certain excitement, and often whispered about what sex must be like. By now Roma and I had already started to read *True Romance* magazines so we had an idea of what sex was about. Roma and I also listened to rude, sexy calypsos like "What is Catty, Big Boy asked; What is Catty, Teacher; Rude Boy want to know, Rude Boy want to know; What is Catty?" We only did this when Mama went out to the shop.

I was always ashamed of my body. I started out as a fairly chubby little girl who quickly grew to what I always thought of as a long and lanky woman — skinny with small breasts. Like my peers, we bought a liquid called Weight-On so I could gain weight. When that didn't work, I would roll my slip up at the sides to create the illusion of hips. The model for how I should look came from Archie comics and the females in it, Veronica and Betty. These were beautiful white ladies with Coke-bottle figures and long hair, neither of which I had. My hair did not grow to even shoulder length. Then there was my complexion. My sisters were lighter skinned than I am. In Shirley's case, she also had a cute turned-up nose, similar to the ladies in the comics. Roma and I thought that Shirley was special, not only as the firstborn, but because she was pretty and did well in school.

When my period came for the first time I panicked. As a result of my upbringing, my background was peculiarly puritanical. I had a sense of isolation as not only the darkest in the family, but also the middle one who should not have been born (my mother having told me that by the time she was pregnant with me, her marriage was over and the last thing she had wanted was another child), the one who cried at the drop of a hat. There was so much repression in the household that I had not been told what my period was, so at first I told no one of this strange, new development. I thought I must have done something wrong; but what? Eventually, when this liquid that I presumed was blood continued to flow, I was forced to tell my mother. I thought I was dying.

My mother's reaction was mystifying. I had never seen such a look on her face. It was a combination of astonishment, fear and a desire to flee. At first she just stood there not speaking. Then she said, 'Go and talk to your sister Shirley.' What on earth could this be, that my mother was unwilling to talk to me about? At least Mama hadn't beaten me. I rushed to Shirley who, in reply to my questions, said, 'Beverley Anderson, I hope you know you can now get pregnant.' The link was thus made between this horrible stuff coming out of me and getting pregnant. It was bad news. Was there nothing I could do not to get pregnant? It seemed not. I now had to be more perfect than ever. I was 12 years old and my life could be ending. That is what pregnancy did. It ended your life. I knew that pregnancy was the outcome for teenage girls who misbehaved, and since misbehaviour, as defined by my mother, covered almost everything, I was in trouble.

At this stage of our growing up, my mother could not bring herself to talk to us about what was happening to our bodies. Later she would explain to me only how to keep myself clean. In those days we used finely woven 'bird's-eye' cotton napkins, which were not disposable and had to be washed after each use. I remember dozens of these 'blood cloths' being washed on a regular basis, especially after my sister Roma started to see her period and my mother had cloths to wash for three daughters. As with our washrags, my mother never trusted us to launder our own napkins. So she ended up doing it all herself. There was a small, white, enamel basin kept for this purpose only. The minute we took the napkins off they had to be placed in this basin in cold water. This was important as it prevented the cloth from getting too stained. She would then add laundry detergent and Dettol and the cloths would be soaked overnight in a corner of the bathroom. The next day the basin would be placed in the sun, and after that the napkins would be hand-washed and left soaking in the sun one more time. Then they would be rinsed and hung on the clothesline. Once dry, they were taken from off the line and carefully folded diagonally, the way we would wear them, ready for use the next month. Because there were three of us, the sight of these napkins swaying in the wind was constant. What a blessing it was when disposables were invented!

Walking the half-hour to school at this time of the month would bring tears to my eyes. We were not allowed to miss days from school. My mother did not believe in succumbing to illness or 'feeling sick'. Whatever we were feeling, we had to proceed as if all was well. I can still feel the wet bird's-eye soaked with blood between my legs, rolling from side to side and often chafing me. I had to adjust my legs so that the walk was less uncomfortable, and keep checking my clothing to ensure that no blood had leaked through. Only 'slack girls' would allow their period to show on their outer garments, or have an odour associated with that time of the month. Then there was the pain: the feeling of your tummy moving around with cramps. A strange type of pain deep down in your belly. My mother kept a bottle of specially prepared 'rice bitters' for these times. She brewed the liquid from a bitter herb and forced us to take it. Sometimes the pain was so bad that we were happy to do so. I hated my period. What had women done to deserve this 'curse' that men never had to endure?

The arrival of my period led to admonitions from my mother about life and sexuality. She gave us several warnings — what I now call her 'sex education lecturettes'. She told us that only slack girls would allow a man to jump on top of them when they were having their periods. Clearly we were never to be that type of girl or woman. 'Slack' was a very negative thing with my mother.

After Franklin Town, I joined Shirley at an Anglican school, St Hugh's High for Girls. Both my parents were against a co-educational school. I am not sure why Daddy chose St Hugh's, but perhaps because it was considered a good Anglican school with British standards.

Once, during high school, I remember hearing my parents having a particularly noisy quarrel, and then suddenly there was silence. Roma, Shirley and I crept together to their room. Maybe this was the night, we thought. Maybe one of them was dead. We saw my father lying flat on his back on the bed with my mother astride him. In her hand she had a kitchen knife. We knew this knife well; she often used the handle to beat us. As she held the knife and cursed him, she said, 'You will never move my children from St Hugh's and send them to Kingston Technical School — not my children. Technical is not good enough for them and they won't get the opportunities they deserve.' She then told him to repeat after her, *'I will not move the children from St Hugh's.'* He repeated the words after her in a quiet, frightened voice. She removed the knife from his neck and climbed off him.

When we realised that Mama was not going to kill him that night, we hurriedly returned to our bed, not uttering a sound in case she heard us. Later we would overhear her talking to herself, or to my father — we were never sure which, because she talked to herself a lot — saying that whenever he had a new sweetheart she would get less house money; and that no sweetheart was going to take away from her children's welfare. The following day she said to our father, 'Don't make me have to put on my clothes and go to see the headmistress of St Hugh's and tell her what you were planning to do.' Mama seldom went to the school, but this time she did. She enlisted the full support of the headmistress in convincing my father to keep us at St Hugh's. As frightened as we were, we felt proud of my mother for standing up for us in this way.

Our three-bedroom home above the railway station always had a distinct smell of train grease and smoke, along with the stench of cattle waiting to be transported. There was also the smell of molasses and the sweet, slightly rotting smell of sugar cane. In those days the rotting trains ran at all hours, transporting cane across the country.

The sound of one arriving in the dead of night would wake us from our sleep. As it came into the station, our home would vibrate. My mother would awaken my father and give him something to drink as he made his way downstairs to tend to the arriving train. The other sound that became a way of life for us was that of the telegraph machine operated by my father, *tick, tick, tick,* with his energetic fingers tapping like crazy. That was how employees of the railway system communicated. Later in life when Daddy got Parkinson's disease and his hands never stopped shaking, I would recall how those fingers had danced on the telegraph machine.

When I arrived at St Hugh's, Shirley had already been there for a year and Roma joined us a year later. Roma and I had only the vaguest idea from Shirley of what the school was like. Our uniforms were stiffly starched, dark green two-piece suits with skirts pleated at the front and back but not at the sides. We wore brown laced-up shoes and socks, and white jippi-jappa straw hats that were 'whitened' constantly so they looked 'spic and span'. When we sweated, drops of sweat combined with the whitening and dropped onto our shoulders. But what I remember most about these uniforms was the large bloomers with elastic in the legs and belted at the waist. Our skinny legs stuck out from beneath the skirts. Underneath our skirts we wore bloomers, designed to hide our private parts. Apparently slips alone were not good enough, perhaps because slips often showed below skirts. Also, the way the uniforms were designed, we could easily remove our skirts and be ready for physical education and games. On those days we carried our white 'creps', our sneakers, in our school bags, as we were not allowed to wear them outside the school grounds. I hated those uniforms. Because of them, children of other schools called the girls of St Hugh's 'green lizards'.

Perhaps bloomers were an additional way to keep our virginity, and everything associated with it, intact. Our headmistress, Rita Landale, and our teachers told us often that St Hugh's girls had a particular type of personality. They obeyed rules and strove for excellence and perfection. Our school song, in honour of the man for whom the school was named, opened with these lines: *'St Hugh of old was wise and bold; a Bishop of renown …'.* We sang it with fervour every morning during assembly.

Shirley, Roma and I were instructed to go straight home from school. There was to be no idling on the streets and we could not do errands in our school uniforms. I had three close friends during my years there, but no best friend. Friendships were difficult for me because we lived so far away. We had other friends who travelled on the train but we were the only ones attending St Hugh's. News spread quickly throughout the school that the Anderson girls had to travel by train from Old Harbour.

The final stop for the train in Kingston was at the railway station, its headquarters at the end of Barry Street. We always prepared our entrances and exit, yet no matter how we readied ourselves, it was always stressful. We didn't like arriving at school late — it was a major embarrassment — so we would leave the train in a hurry. Shirley was a fast walker and always got off to a running start, Roma and I following behind her, giggling at the way she walked, with her heavy bag making her appear oddly twisted, one shoulder higher than the other. The giggling slowed us down considerably but we couldn't stop it. We would walk to Parade, where the buses were parked, and then take a bus to Cross Roads, the location of the school. When we got off the bus, there was more walking. By the time we arrived, assembly would be underway in the school hall.

The hall was located at the bottom of what we called a 'hill', so the other students who had arrived earlier saw us through the building's open sides, walking quickly, but not running. We had to join a 'late line', which was immediately in front of the high platform on which the headmistress and teachers sat. My parents tried to get the headmistress to excuse us for being late every morning and to prevent us from being embarrassed in this way, but to no avail. The headmistress insisted that we obey the rules of the school and stand in that awful line.

Another source of embarrassment for us at St Hugh's was the coconut cakes. Every night my mother stayed up late after she had finished her other chores and made these cakes, the proceeds of which were intended to supplement our bus fares. I remember her stirring the coconut, which she had grated by hand, with sugar and water. Steam poured out of the deep covered pan. When the mixture was ready she would drop spoonfuls of the mixture onto a platter, where they were left to cool and harden. The next morning she would package them and give each of us our share to sell at school. It was hard work for her, and harder for us. But the other girls loved them and we usually sold them all and the teachers never objected. However embarrassed we were to be known as the children who had to sell coconut cakes in order to afford to stay at school, my mother declared that it was an honest living, and that we should never be ashamed of making an honest living.

We carried our lunch from Old Harbour because it was cheaper to do so and Mama couldn't afford the school canteen. Our set lunch was sandwiches made of cheese and jam. We also drank fresh cow's milk, which we got from an adjoining farm operated by Carl Marsh, who owned the plantation next to the railway. We had a little of the lunch during the school break and most of it after school while we waited for the train. By the time we got to the lunch after school, it was evident that it had been shut up in the lunch pan for a while.

The train left Old Harbour at 5:30 a.m. and we returned home by 7:00 p.m. or later, in the sugar-cane season and we had to wait for the sugar-cane trains to clear the tracks before the passenger train was allowed through. By the time we got home during cane season we had finished our homework on the train, and Mama just made us go to the bathroom and to bed — to sleep and wake up to begin yet another day.

Shirley's best friend at St Hugh's was Sonja Harris. We never understood why she spelled her name that way but were intrigued by it. She came from a home with two professional parents — her mother, Irene, was a teacher who had taught us at Franklin Town Primary, and her father, Jack, had known my mother before she was married and there was talk that he had once been in love with her. The Harrises — Sonja, her cousin Faye, and her parents — lived at Lacy Road in Franklin Town in a lovely home of their own. Sometimes after school we would go there to wait for the train. Mrs Harris took good care of us. We would have our snack and listen to records; at that time the Platters were popular. Roma and I felt honoured to be in the company of the big girls like Shirley and Sonja. I remember envying Sonja when her breasts started to grow. One day she made us look at her brassiere. We were all flat-chested like Mama and we were all skinny, including Sonja. We enjoyed those afternoons at Lacy Road. And we never once missed the train in all those years of travelling.

In high school, there were times when we each had only one uniform. Every evening my mother would wash and iron these uniforms so that it appeared that we had one for each day of the week. Often the uniforms would be patched on the hips, and although my mother's patches were as neat as possible, this could be embarrassing.

I was an average student and never quite understood why it was important to study subjects like mathematics and history. What use would they be to someone who would probably end up as a wife, who might probably also turn out to be a secretary, a nurse or a teacher? It was fear of my mother and constant reminders of how she was sacrificing her very life to send me to school that made me do any studying at all. I loved English literature and hated maths, and was a good drama student. My favourite poem, for which I won annual elocution contests, was Wordsworth's 'Ode to a Daffodil'. Whenever I was on stage reciting this poem I was transformed from a quiet, shy and inhibited child who cried easily, into someone from whom came this powerful voice that made each word ring. I still remember the opening lines of the poem: 'I wandered lonely as a cloud that floats on high o'er vales and hills ... when all at once I saw a crowd — a host of golden daffodils.' When I said these words I would feel lifted outside of myself as I, too, floated like the clouds. For me, drama was a healing tool. I loved the experience of being someone or something else. I also wondered about these flowers called daffodils that seemed to grow everywhere in this far-off place called England. What did they really look like? In appreciating poetry I was using a part of my brain that I didn't use often and I enjoyed that. Years later when I arrived in London for the first time, it was spring and the daffodils were blooming everywhere, as in the poem — 'beside the lake, beyond the trees' — and I was finally able to put poem and reality together. My days at Franklin Town were numbered, however, as I soon received a scholarship to St Hugh's High School for girls.

Our headmistress, a 'high brown' lady with good hair — she looked like a female version of Martin Luther from our history books — was distressed at this turn of events. She was rumoured to have said she could not preside over a school that was going to the dogs because of all these 'scholarship girls'. There was discrimination from other members of the staff too. Miss Kingdom, the librarian, reminded me of a dragon. She was tall, with huge legs and feet, and wispy hair, and she referred to the library as 'My library'. We, the scholarship girls, always knew that the teachers preferred the high brown girls and white girls, who kept to themselves unless they needed help with their homework. To be black, working class and have 'bad hair' meant you had three strikes against you.

The only scandal I can remember at school was when a girl my age got pregnant. She came to school for a while during the rumours and we watched her as she gained weight and her breasts grew. Her personality too seemed to change, it soured as she developed. Eventually she left school and we never heard of her again. This reinforced in me my mother's teachings about sin, sex and pregnancy.

I couldn't wait to leave St Hugh's and get on with my life, and so, at 16 years old, I did. My mother was anxious to have more money available for the family, and I was happy to be finished with classes and homework. By then, Daddy had been transferred to Spanish Town. There was no residence for the stationmaster there, so my parents rented first a small house and then a larger one; rentals there were far cheaper than in Kingston. Shirley was completing A levels and about to enter the University of the West Indies. It was always clear to us that the family would only be able to afford to send the firstborn to university. I had no difficulty with that, as university was of no interest to me at the time. I just wanted economic independence so that I could leave home. I knew there was a life beyond my mother's house and I was anxious to begin my adventures. But not even I could attempt to move out of the house before I was 21. That was another four and a half years away.

Daddy insisted that before taking a job, I should do a commercial course in shorthand and typing, and so I was ready to begin my professional career as a secretary. I got a temporary job at the Parish Council of St Catherine in Spanish Town, the seat of local government in that parish, which was located in the historical square. I was lucky to get into a department headed by the CEO of the council, George Lewars. The department had three extraordinarily gifted women in it — Cynthia Blair, Joyce Bolton and Maisie O'Reggio. Joyce would later head the council, and Maisie would move to the civil service and become a permanent secretary in the Ministry of Youth. These ladies took me under their wing.

George Lewars was a perfectionist. His job was to ensure the efficient running of the council, which included giving councillors and members of parliament who were ex-officio members of the council detailed notes of each regular council meeting and subcommittee meeting. Joyce Bolton, as the senior person in the office, went to these meetings and took verbatim notes in shorthand, which she then transcribed and put in order for Mr Lewars. Mistakes were not allowed. Mr Lewars would then use those notes as source material to dictate them back to Joyce. Joyce's typing was magical to me, and I loved to watch her fingers fly over the keys, and hear the quick-tempoed music they made.

Once the minutes were finished, any action needed was speedily carried out. To make this simple, one copy of the minutes was cut up into separate sections and pasted onto blank sheets of paper with an action memo from Mr Lewars typed under each decision. This is where I came in. If there was an item in the minutes to do with Riversdale Water Supply, I would cut the relevant section from the minutes and paste it onto a letter-size piece of plain paper. Then I would type in a memo directed to the relevant officer. Mr Lewars would sometimes dictate the memo, or, if it was a simple referral for attention, I would just type it in. Once Mr Lewars had signed it, it went off to the relevant officer, but before this, everything about the movement of that memo was noted in a hard-cover full-sized scrapbook, so that we could trace the correspondence. I learned about order and discipline from that Parish Council job, where no mistakes were allowed.

I enjoyed my position there, and after a few months I got much more involved in the taking of notes and preparing the minutes. I got to know the mayor, who was the political head of the council, and some of the councillors well. Sometimes, just for the fun of it, I would go with the members of parliament into their constituencies. At the time I joined the council, the People's National Party was in office, but was soon replaced by the Jamaica Labour Party. I did not distinguish between the two, despite having come out of a PNP family.

This then was my second taste of politics, and it was different from the political meetings of my childhood. Now I was able to see what a constituency was like and how it was organised, and the critical role local government played in dealing with the needs of each individual. I also saw the relationship between the MP and his constituents in rural Jamaica. A representative had to deal with a whole range of issues. I was fascinated by this life and I loved communicating with farmers who lived so close to the soil. I gave everything to my job and was not content merely to sit in the office but preferred to get out in the field. I worked long, hard hours. It was expected of me. And it was the only way to get the work done well. I was also happy not to be home very much. My pay cheque was handed over to my mother and, as more money flowed in, things at home eased a great deal. For the first time, we weren't living solely off my father's salary. Roma left school after her Senior Cambridge, having done only one year of A levels, and she too started to work. So, by then, my mother's dream was coming true — she had two working daughters. It was time to buy a car so that when Shirley went to university, although she would live on campus in a residence hall, a vehicle would be available to her.

During my two years or so at the council, I learned many skills that have stayed with me to this day. I became an efficient secretary with good shorthand and typing skills; I learned about politics at the local government level; I saw politicians at work; I gained an understanding of the dynamics of organisation; I learned how to defend myself from sexual harassment on the job — and I was beginning to accept that I was intelligent and attractive to men, though for a long time I didn't know what to make of this.

By the early 1960s, the JLP was again in power. The PNP lost the referendum which was called to decide whether Jamaica should stay in the Caribbean Federation. When Norman Manley had seen how hostile the JLP was to the Federation, he felt it was necessary to get the view of the voters. Several discussions took place inside the PNP and Manley was advised not to go the route of a referendum, as the results would be along partisan lines. However, he went ahead with it.

When the PNP lost the referendum, Manley, again against the wishes of the party, called a general election so that the Jamaican people could decide which party they wanted to lead them into political independence. The people chose the JLP. Two of the MPs on the council, Roy McNeill and Johnnie Gyles were selected as cabinet ministers. The former was named minister of home affairs and the latter minister of agriculture. They had both become my good friends. The mayor, Roy McNeil, had made me an offer to go to the ministry with him as his secretary, but I was not willing to take that step. My PNP bona fides were too strong and I thought it would kill Daddy. I realised it was time for me to move on and, despite protests from my mother, I did. Without knowing where I was going next, I resigned from the Parish Council.

Little did I know that 10 years after the referendum, the next time the PNP came to office, Norman Manley's son would be prime minister and party leader, and my life would shift in an extraordinary way.

Chapter 3

In the mid-1960s I was one of a group of Jamaicans who went to London to complete production work on a film starring Anthony Quinn and James Coburn, *A High Wind in Jamaica*. Vista Productions Limited, owned by Perry Henzell, was the Jamaican partner on the film. I was Perry's film production assistant and my job in Jamaica had been, among other things, local casting. Twentieth Century Fox had taken over the Runaway Bay Hotel to house actors and crew for six months because the film location was close by, at Rio Bueno. We set up a makeshift dressing room for Anthony on location and in between takes he would tell us wonderful stories about his life, and discuss philosophy. I struck up a great friendship with him then, and later, and when we were in London after completion of the film, Barbara, my sister, Roma, and I saw him one night walking in Earl's Court. Quinn's face was partially covered because he didn't want to be recognised, but for us there was no mistaking who he was. He spoke to us and we were thrilled.

In London I shared a flat with Roma, who was already living there, and Barbara Blake, a Jamaican journalist whose father, also a journalist, was well known in Jamaica. Barbara would later become the first black person on the BBC. It was the 1960s, and London, England, was the first place in which I was to come face to face with racism. Before that, it had been something I had only read about. It had nothing to do with me, or so I thought. I did not even know that the way my mother had treated me, because I was the darkest in our family, had anything to do with racism. That was just the way mothers were. We had searched for a flat in as fashionable a place as we could afford with our combined means, and had not anticipated any problems. But we always got the same response — no vacancies. It was not unusual at that time to see signs saying, NO COLOUREDS OR DOGS ALLOWED. White people still stared at blacks. The movie *To Sir with Love* starring Sidney Poitier was popular then, and after seeing it, I remember walking along the street and looking into shop windows and, for the first time, seeing myself as black.

After completion of the film, Barbara, who had a bit part in it, and I decided to stay on in London. Roma was already employed at *The Economist* Intelligence Unit (EIU) and she helped me land a job as secretary to one of the senior managers. This was my first experience seeing research at work, as the unit worked in several countries around the world, gathering economic, political and social data, some of which ended up as background material for *The Economist* magazine. Working at my typewriter, watching events and reporting unfold before me, was fascinating, particularly when a crisis broke out and a researcher from the EIU would be dispatched to report back to head office. Senior staff would move from country to country for short stints as they investigated what was happening in conflict areas. Research became and remains one of my passions.

At the same time I took a course at the London School of Film Technique. After my experience at Vista, I felt that my career would be in film production — though very much behind the camera. I wanted to return to Jamaica with new skills to offer Perry and Vista Productions. At the school, student teams would take to the streets of London and film real-life situations. It was a practical course, but, as it turned out, I would never put these skills to use.

One of the things I always appreciated about Perry was that he taught me what it was like to have a genuine friendship with a man without the involvement of sex. He was very much in love with Sally Densham, though they often broke up. Their relationship gave me an idea of what being in love could be like — two free spirits who could not do without each other but who, in order to stay together, had to be away from each other from time to time, sometimes in different countries. I remember that at one stage Sally, herself a creative person, was the window-dresser for Selfridges in London. Perry and Sally finally got married and had two children, Justine and Jason. Justine now, among other things, coordinates the Calabash Literary Festival. Sally was the first female liberated spirit I knew.

Perry worked long hours on film documentaries and advertisements, but we often went out for lunch or dinner. He was the first person to encourage me to read literature and to explain how this could open up my life. He always told me that I had a good mind and that what I needed to do was to develop it. With other bosses who were men, this was not the case. So I recognised early that my mother was right: the world was organised in the interest of men. Women had to protect themselves and protect their children. But I learned too that there were exceptions to this rule; and Perry was one of them.

I was amazed when a few people began suggesting that I had the looks to be a professional model. For so long I had considered myself ugly. Now I was tall and slim with, some said, an 'interesting' look. I still didn't see myself this way and therefore turned the offers down, yet, in terms of my self-esteem, London was good for me.

But although the city was fascinating, I hungered for home. This was the London of fashion designer Mary Quant, and the singer Lulu of 'Downtown' fame. It was also the London of the Beetles. At the time Nancy Wilson was belting out 'How glad I am', and occasionally we would participate in a live BBC television show where famous artists performed and we danced to the music. I particularly enjoyed stopping at the grocery store and the butcher's on my way home from work to collect dinner and the newspapers. I developed an active social life mainly through the cosmopolitan group that worked at the unit. Yet I felt alienated in London. I was also upset about being so broke that I had to depend on boyfriends to take me out.

While abroad I dated mostly white men. The choice at the unit tended to be between whites and Africans, but I never dated an African. I suppose that was partly because of my socialisation, my mother having warned us when we were growing up that nothing black was good. I was also forewarned by friends who had dated or married black men and had found the cultural divide too wide. Also, to be honest, I found the Africans' customary approaches threatening. I remember one man literally stalking me down Oxford Street, shouting, 'I think

I like you, I think I like you' in a guttural, commanding tone that reminded me of the cinematic stereotype of an African chieftain. Terrified, I dashed into Marks and Spencer, and waited there until I was sure he had passed.

The first day I walked into the unit I saw a tall, handsome Englishman who stopped my breath. Roma told me that he was senior staff member of *The Economist*. 'Knowing you, Beverley', she said, 'he will be dating you in no time'. Her response shocked me, for implicit in what she said was that I held a certain power — a power I had not known I possessed. Within two days Roma's prediction came true. That relationship saved me from loneliness and opened a world to me. The man was from the British upper class, and he took me to upscale restaurants and night clubs. He also introduced me to the finer points of London, from opera to leg of lamb, for he was a man of eclectic tastes, and he was also a fine cook.

Still I missed home. All my money was being spent on our Gloucester Road flat, which left little for anything else. I hated the penury, which reminded me of my childhood, so eventually Roma and I boarded with a couple in Shepherd's Bush to save some money. Living with strangers, however, made us unhappy, and soon, despite my wonderful romantic relationship, I telephoned Perry in Kingston and told him that I needed to return. He generously sent me a London-to-Kingston ticket. He also told me about an exciting project he was working on. He wanted to write, produce and direct Jamaica's first full-length feature film, based on the story of Rhygin, who was the only 'bad man' I could remember from my youth, a sort of Jamaican 'Robin Hood' who achieved notoriety in the 1940s, and was eventually shot by police. My family had been living in Rollington Town when Rhygin was on the prowl and I recall seeing a picture of him on the front page of the *Gleaner* with a gun in each hand. It's an image I have never forgotten. Everyone was fascinated by the fact that the police couldn't catch the man; as kids we would sing, 'Rhygin was here but he just disappear.' Perry planned to use this story to highlight what happens when young boys migrate from rural Jamaica to Kingston in search of a better living. I was excited by the project — which would become the acclaimed *The Harder They Come* — and not surprised that Perry would take this on. He was a man of huge ideas, and a little thing like not knowing where the money would come from didn't faze him. I packed my bags and left London without much of a backward glance, even to my rescuing knight. We stayed in touch for a while, but he was out of place in the Jamaican context and so the relationship didn't last.

On my return I had hardly settled down at Vista Productions, joining Perry in discussions with various groups to flesh out his ideas on the Rhygin story, before a friend of his, Derek Manderson, an advertising executive, paid one of his many visits to the office. He took one look at me and said that I belonged on the television screen. I knew he was crazy. At the time it was difficult for me to even walk across a crowded room without feeling self-conscious, much less think about appearing on television. Theatre was a different matter; because I was playing a part. I protested, but Derek insisted that I do a screen test; he would not give up. It was difficult to resist the man. When I did do the test I was surprised at how well it went. And that was my entrance to the Jamaica Broadcasting Corporation (JBC). Perry Henzell was generous and supportive all the way. He had always seen me as bigger than I saw myself, and so he let me go. Intuitively, he knew I was stepping up.

The JBC had been established by Norman Manley during the first PNP regime in 1957, five years before political independence. Based on the models of the independent British Broadcasting Corporation and Canadian Broadcasting Corporation, the JBC was seen as a vehicle for nation building, one that would allow a formerly colonised people to begin to develop a sense of self, to discuss relevant ideas and issues, and to come to terms with a true, indigenous reality. This in itself was revolutionary, coming at a time when Jamaica had only one radio station, Radio Jamaica Rediffusion (RJR), whose programming was mostly foreign. Norman Manley saw the need for the kind of institution that would involve the best minds in the country. It was to be an extension of the Drumblair Movement, named after Norman and Edna Manley's home, a symbol of the nationalist movement, political and cultural. Intellectuals and artists gathered there, and this extraordinary group had one thing in common — a vision of Jamaica beyond colonialism. They became the pioneers of an independence of mind that is our enduring legacy. Manley was clear that there should be no political interference in JBC, and so in its initial stages the corporation was placed under his portfolio as premier.

The atmosphere in the station in 1969 was tense — reflecting that of the broader society towards the end of that first decade of independence, primarily the result of economic growth without development, and of racial issues. Furthermore, the

JBC always lagged behind RJR in the ratings. Ongoing political interference, largely incompetent and ineffective management that changed on a regular basis, and low staff morale all combined to prevent the station from effectively carrying out its original role. A young British consultant, Michael Bukt, was brought in, in the hope that he could provide a remedy. He was able to mobilise the staff around the slogan 'Big J', and for the first time the JBC began to lead in the ratings. For those of us at the station who continued to do everything to maintain its viability, this new promotion spearheaded by Bukt was a welcome one. Under his leadership, the team performed inside and outside the studios in exemplary ways. As for me, as producer, news reader, host for TV's *Young World* — a music and dance programme similar to those in which I had participated at the BBC Studios — I was busy and learning skills guided by the brightest and the best, including Leonie Forbes, my mentor. I also observed and longed to be like Erica Allen, who was the only person at the time who sold consumer items on television. It was one of the most exciting times of my life.

My memories and experience of the JBC in the 1960s are of a station in which political interference was rampant. In fact, it was not unusual for the prime minister himself to telephone the newsroom. There was a climate of fear. The JBC had begun to be a partisan political football. In spite of this, I developed professional and social relations with many of my colleagues — Desmond Chambers, Neville Willoughby, Uriel Aldridge, Sonia Lazarus, Pat Lazarus, Gladstone Wilson, Jeff Barnes — all duty announcers like myself. It was a truly wonderful team of people. Here was a station that had been developed to capture the creative imagination of the best in Jamaica, yet halfway through its first decade of existence — 1957–1967 — the dream had been deferred. The concept of process, dialectics and change would come to me later in my life. For now, I continued to work at the station, trying to find ways to make a difference. The music of the times — including that of Desmond Dekker and the Aces, who sang about poverty — became one of our most important tools.

One of the most exciting and revelatory experiences I had at JBC came from my involvement with such musicians, who gave me a glimpse of a totally different way of life and made me realise how sheltered mine had been. I grew up in a family where my father received a paycheque every week. Through the genius of my mother, the money stretched and, as long as we were careful, we never went hungry. I had read Orlando Patterson's *Children of Sisyphus,* which set out conditions in the ghetto in a graphic but literal way. Orlando and I had been friends from our teenage years, and had partied together. We knew him as Horace. The image that stayed with many people, including me, from this, his first novel, was one of men, women and children rummaging through garbage for food to eat. Now, through the songs of young Jamaican musicians, I saw the horror of real poverty. One of the songs of the period that had enormous influence on me was 'Johnny yu too bad' — 'Walking down the street with the pistol in yu hand / Johnny yu too bad.'

The music of the early 1960s was revolutionary, not so much in the lyrics but in the sound itself. Heavily influenced by the Rastafarian culture, the music represented in a profound way the uniting of Jamaicans with their homeland Africa. It represented a return trip to the homeland — the spiritual migration back to Africa. I found it fascinating getting to know these artists as they struggled to have their music heard on air. I often went to dances and this was also the time of the new sound systems. Artists such as Desmond Dekker and the Aces, Derrick Harriott, Dobby Dobson, the Techniques, Lee Scratch Perry, Prince Buster, Justin Hinds, Bob Andy, and Hopeton Lewis were some of the more popular ones. I remember Bob Marley and the Wailers hanging out under a tree in the JBC yard singing and playing their music, hoping for an opportunity to appear on television. Later, at PNP headquarters, I reasoned with Peter Tosh for a while almost daily. There was much anger and deep hurt in him; I have never met anyone so ready to both implode and explode.

When I first started at JBC I had a number of duties. I was one of several people responsible for reading the news on air, on radio and later on TV. I was also involved in production for both radio and television. Leonie Forbes must have been in her thirties when I arrived at JBC without any training whatsoever in either radio or television. She was an interesting and talented actress and producer, and had just returned from studying in London. She was one of the few women who had undergone systematic training in theatre. My first impression of her was of a generous but no-nonsense professional. When I got to know her, I recognised that we shared the idea that we could be perfect in everything that we did. So our work together began. She had carved out a small office space for herself, a long, narrow, windowless passage adjoining the canteen. There were no other offices nearby. On one wall was the sound and editing equipment. We had only two small desks but we made the space as attractive as possible. We also had a portable tape recorder for on-the-street, vox-pop-type interviews. There was a great deal of work to be done and in that small, almost claustrophobic space, as I got to know the business first hand, we got to know each other well.

Leonie and I both wanted to develop programmes that would reach out meaningfully to Jamaicans in their everyday lives. Together we co-hosted and co-produced *Jamaica Woman*, a radio programme that dealt with issues important to the working woman. We explored problems such as poor road conditions, water supply shortages, inadequate garbage collection, particularly as these affected women in their traditional roles in the household.

While working on this programme, I had my first experience of institutional discrimination. It was not unusual for the then chairman of the board to summon us to his office in downtown Kingston if he felt that we had criticised the government in any way. One morning, while on air broadcasting the radio programme *Jamaica Woman,* a listener asked me to mention that the garbage in her area had not been collected for weeks. I did so. Soon after, the general manager, Merrick Needham, called me into his office and told me that the chairman wanted to see me about certain statements I had made.

When I walked into the chairman's office, he made himself absolutely clear. The station would not tolerate any statements that could be seen as anti-government. It was obvious that he had received a telephone call from someone in a position of power. I could not tell him what I was really thinking — that the JLP administration was destroying the station through this kind of partisan political interference. I really wanted to tell him to go to hell, even if it meant accepting the consequences. He was a rich, brown, JLP lawyer with, what I perceived to be, the kind of power that had for so long victimised so many. My tribal instincts came to the fore: I knew that my party, the PNP, would never conduct business in this disgraceful way. Nevertheless, I meekly promised to be more careful about what I said on air. I knew then that it would be only a matter of time before I left the JBC, for it would stifle my creativity. And the incident stayed with me.

Leonie and I also created a Jamaica Woman Coffee Club: every Saturday morning we met with a group in one of the JBC studios and facilitated conversations about matters important to them. We taped these discussions and played them back during the week on our programme. The segments became very popular. Discussions centred around the roles and responsibilities of women and therefore the issues that affected them in their daily lives — the state of roads, water shortages, caring for children and the elderly — the kind of issues that were largely the responsibility of central and local government. Many of these issues therefore related to the Kingston and St Andrew Corporation (KSAC) and the Parish Councils. I had become accustomed to voices complaining about roads or water supplies when I worked at the St Catherine Parish Council in the early 1960s. It was not unusual then for women and men to march in anger, ready to attack the staff because they had been without water for days, weeks or even months. Although I did not realise it at the time, these were political issues and ones that made the government of the day, the JLP, look bad. Given that the JBC was then seen as an arm of the government, this provided Leonie and I with problems from time to time, as there were complaints to the chairman of the Board. But as far as Leonie and I were concerned, what we were doing was innovative radio, and politics never entered our minds.

In preparation for the Jamaica Woman Coffee Club, we organised seats in a circle to make it easier for women to see and connect with each other. Sponsors provided the coffee, pastries and juice and it was a wonderful social occasion. After a while, we started receiving an increasing number of requests from people to participate. The taped on-air sessions slowly began to have an impact, as political representatives and policy makers responded to the needs articulated on the programme. I was beginning to realise the extent to which some issues were the sole concern of women. Women did the household chores whether they had jobs or not. They also looked after not only the very young, but the very old as well. It seemed they did everything, and because they were not paid for the household tasks they performed, critical as those roles and responsibilities were, they were financially dependent on men.

Leonie and I also adopted a West Kingston charity, Operation Friendship, and collected foodstuff and clothes to help alleviate some suffering. This institution was led by Rev Webster Edwards and focused on children. Edward Seaga, someone with whom my life would be inextricably joined in years to come, represented the constituency of West Kingston. Leonie and I never saw the programme as partisan, however; we just wanted to help the children.

After a while, a young student named Cecile Wilson interned with us. She did odd jobs, mostly running up and down between our office and the sound library upstairs. Cecile helped us to find appropriate music for the programme. She would later rise to the position of librarian. Long after I left JBC, Cecile and I remained friends, up until her death. I also developed an extraordinary relationship with members of the operating and technical staff. When we came off duty, we often packed up and went to the beach. We got along well, and that was important because, to a large extent, they could determine how you sounded on air. It was not unusual for them to cut you off if they thought you sounded stupid. This was a group of highly qualified and competent young men, many of whom later migrated to the United States or Canada and were successful there.

For me, the most exciting aspect of the work was editing sound tape. In those days we had to cut the tape with an editing knife, and Leonie taught me how to create miracles. I was particularly intrigued by what was involved if we wanted to take out a short breath or sound that we didn't want to be heard. As we edited, long streams of tape flowed down the side of the sound machine, curling up and ending in circles on the floor. We would work for hours and hours on weekdays and weekends to get a five or 15-minute interview just right. I learned tolerance and resilience from Leonie, watching the way she stayed with the process long after I had got bored. She became like a big sister to me. When she got married, I even lived in her house for a while.

Working in media gave me a new concept of time. No matter what the time of day or night, the demands of the job came first. I remember the night that Martin Luther King died. I was in a studio editing tape and someone from the newsroom rushed in and said that King had died and they didn't have a newsman to go to Jamaica House to get a response from Prime Minister Shearer. He handed me a tape recorder and off I went. This would be my first visit to Jamaica House. I had no way of knowing that it would one day be my home. I remember noticing the long driveway and circular stairs. We were led through an outdoor garden area to a formal living room where the prime minister was already talking to journalists. I had seen him in person before but never this close. A tall, striking man with mischievous-looking eyes, ever ready to flirt — that was my first impression of Prime Minister Shearer. After telling me that he wanted me to make him sound good, his press attaché, Hartley Neita, a handsome and genuinely charming man who quickly put me at ease, handed him a brief and I began to record his voice.

Although I never worked in the newsroom I remember it as the scene of ongoing activity, 24 hours a day. The news runner would race into the studio from the downstairs newsroom mere minutes before the programme went on air. There was always a sense of urgency and some degree of apprehension on my part as I accepted the newsprint from him. I had to be a perfectionist; making mistakes while reading the news was not acceptable. As I read, I was ever aware of the face of the technical operator on the other side of the separating pane of glass. He would not hesitate to chastise me if I made a mistake on his watch. I listened to the BBC news several times each day so that I correctly pronounced the foreign places and names.

At the time, my parents lived in Port Antonio where my father had been transferred as stationmaster. Again they lived above the railway station. Port Antonio is the capital of Portland, the most naturally beautiful parish in Jamaica. It was not unusual for me to sign off the television station at midnight, get together some friends and take off for the two-and-a-half-hour drive to Port Antonio to spend the weekend. I always kept a pillowcase packed with necessities in the trunk of my car. Surprisingly, my mother enjoyed these visits and took good care of all of us.

There was never a dull moment at JBC. When Guyanese historian Walter Rodney's advocacy of the working poor prompted Prime Minister Shearer to ban him from returning to Jamaica, protests broke out. During the Rodney protests of October 1968, university students took to the streets. So did the police — with tear gas. For three days there was chaos and fear. Not since 1938 had Jamaica seen anything like this. Not only did I read the news, I experienced it. And the JBC was embroiled in a related controversy. Why, yet again, was the prime minister so involved with how we reported the news? At the beginning of the decade of independence it had been the JBC strike, and now it was the Rodney protests. Again the politicians were interfering instead of leaving it to the station to handle the coverage.

At JBC we carried on. I had the opportunity through my work to meet and converse with people from all walks of life, both on and off the air. My confidence grew as my skills improved, and I gained a certain understanding of the power of media — discovering that listeners actually cared deeply about what was said on radio and television, that through our broadcasts we were able to reach out to people across the country, and that, in an odd way, they felt that they owned us, the media 'celebrities'. Eventually I could go nowhere without being recognised. The loss of my anonymity was scary and thrilling at the same time.

I had just been appointed programme manager for radio when Norman Manley's youngest son, Michael, walked into my life. It was a Friday morning and the general manager, Wycliffe Bennett, had asked me to see him. He told me that Manley was coming into the station the following morning to record a broadcast for the National Workers Union, the union affiliated with the PNP and to which JBC workers belonged.

Michael Manley was already legendary there in a way that would someday reflect his often controversial personality. A few years earlier, as the union's island supervisor, he had endeared himself to the public by taking a dramatic stand during the JBC strike, which had erupted when the JBC governing board fired two members of the newsroom team, George Lee and Adrian Rodway, for reporting a news story about a union meeting on wage negotiations. Lee was fired for filing the story and Rodway was fired over a technical glitch, for putting the story on air without first getting the permission of his senior editor. In protest, Michael Manley had lain down on a Kingston street, refusing to move, even when an army vehicle threatened to roll over him and other strikers. When I arrived at the JBC years later, this story was still very much alive in the station's institutional memory.

But another incident that rustled through the station's rumour vine was far less flattering to Michael Manley. In the divorce between Reggie Carter, a prominent JBC TV, radio and drama personality, and his wife Barbara Lewars Carter, Manley had been named as the co-respondent. In those days details of divorces were dutifully published in the daily newspapers. I was working at the station when the divorce news broke in the daily *Star*. Hearing about the proceedings left an unpleasant taste in my mouth. Also, Reggie lived down the road from the flat I then shared with Audrey Chong, a senior producer and presenter for the Jamaica Information Service, whose offices were adjoining the JBC. Reggie would often visit us at night, crying over the Michael and Barbara matter. What manner of man was this Michael Manley? I was soon to find out.

My only other opinion of Manley was that he sounded boring on radio. If I was the duty announcer when a taped broadcast came on from him, I would introduce it and promptly go to sleep. The technical operator would wake me up when he was about to finish so that I could present the 'back' — end of broadcast — announcement. Manley sounded so dull, so old. And now Wycliffe was asking me to produce this particular broadcast — on my day off, no less — because the person normally responsible for it was ill.

I begged Wycliffe not to make this request of me, especially for a Saturday morning. I had no interest whatsoever in producing Michael Manley. From what I had heard of him, he was not someone I wanted to meet. He was, after all, the quintessential playboy — the type my mother had warned her daughters about. But Wycliffe stood firm.

The following morning I awoke and reluctantly got out of bed. Despite my lack of enthusiasm for the assignment, I got to the station early and waited for Manley downstairs at the entrance. He was driving himself in some kind of fancy American car. He parked and jumped out like an athlete. I was aware immediately of long legs and what appeared to be an unusually long torso. The way he wore his clothes emphasised this; his plaid short-sleeve shirt was tucked neatly into his Levi's, revealing a not-too-wide leather belt. His wavy hair was brushed neatly down on his head. He looked every bit the playboy. Yet he seemed to have a perpetual frown and was obviously under stress. I imagined it was because his wife, Barbara, was at the time dying of cancer. This was public knowledge. I was cautious of him, but felt some sympathy for what he must be going through.

He was in a hurry and recorded the broadcast as if he just wanted to get it over with. So did I, but the resulting recording was awful. To my surprise, when I met him in the narrow passageway outside the studio to say goodbye, he looked me in the eye and asked me, in an urgent voice, how it sounded. 'How was that ... was it okay?' In reply I blurted out, in my customary way, without thinking, 'No, it was terrible.' He stuttered a surprised response and asked me if I had really meant that. I said that I did. Manley asked if there was anything he could do about it. He looked genuinely concerned and said that no one had ever been so candid about one of his broadcasts before and he had always thought he was doing fine. I told him that if he had time, I could play the recording back so he could listen and decide for himself. After hearing it, he agreed with my assessment. Although he didn't have much time, he asked what could be done to improve it. He explained that he was on his way to rural Jamaica where a bauxite strike was threatening. I replied that I needed at least half an hour.

We sat down and listened to the tape again, going through some of the worst sections. I quickly taught him how to 'colour' his words so that they would jump off the page and how to vary his voice to keep listeners' attention. I explained how to introduce and end the broadcast effectively and how to keep his audience in mind — addressing them directly and understanding their points of view. We re-wrote some sections of the broadcast to make it more media friendly, choosing words that were more appropriate for radio than print.

When he did the rerecording and listened again, he was amazed and so was I. What a difference! I had never worked with anyone who learned these communication skills so quickly and easily. He was a natural. He fell in love with this new delivery and was like a child who had just made a discovery. He said he would ask his close friends to listen so that he could get feedback. Although I did not admit it at the time, his reaction intrigued me. Here was this man — a Manley — who had already distinguished himself in the trade union movement and on the country as a whole, and yet he was willing to humble himself and learn communication techniques from a young woman. The next day one of his close associated called me about giving him private lessons.

These lessons lasted an hour each. One of my conditions was that we approach the sessions professionally and that he not flirt with me, and he kept his part of the agreement. I would tape him and then we would both listen and assess it; we often taped the same segment again and again, as many times as it took for us to see the improvement we wanted. These techniques would of course become even more critical for him later in his career. I will admit, I was impressed by Manley. I had never met anyone quite like him. It did not occur to me that there was a chance of a relationship, however — after all, we came from different social classes, he'd already been married three times, and then there was his age.

In many ways the JBC, as Norman Manley envisioned it — as a means of communication for the national movement, one that would give the people a sense of self, and aid in nation building — and the JBC strike would become case studies for the kind of leadership and society that Michael Manley aspired to create. Justice and equality were twin concepts that underpinned everything he would do politically at the national, regional and international levels. To that had to be added the fact that his sense of 'bottom-up' planning and ensuring that whoever was involved in the struggle — in the case of the JBC strike, the delegates and workers — had a voice in the decision-making process. He was well aware of the importance of mobilising those involved and keeping them committed. Manley was up against a powerful JLP administration, a JLP-led board of directors, a minister of information in the person of Edward Seaga, and the turbulent environment of the 1960s, that first decade of independence during which, in many ways, the people's rights were trampled. Through it all came the outcry for black power and social justice. The JBC strike paved the way for many of the struggles that Jamaicans would take up in the second decade of independence.

My JBC experiences helped enormously in laying a foundation and preparing me for where I would go next. They were exciting days in radio, television, modelling and theatre. My flatmate Audrey taught me how to entertain, and so we socialised in our charming apartment at least once weekly, extending invitations to women and men in our world. It was not unusual for me to complete a television show, proceed to a modelling assignment on a cruise liner, the *Starward,* and then appear in a theatrical production the following night.

I had no idea then that within months of my first encounter with Michael Manley, our lives would begin to interwine.

Chapter 4

On Norman Washington Manley's 75th birthday, July 4, 1968, members of the People's National Party crammed the 6,000-seat National Arena to say goodbye to their beloved leader and founder. It was more than symbolic that his farewell function should take place here, in the arena adjoining Jamaica's National Stadium. The stadium complex had been erected under his administration when Sir Herbert McDonald, a sportsman and public servant, persuaded Manley to build it. One of the often repeated Manley family stories told how at the time of independence when the stadium was opened, the JLP administration had spurned Norman Manley.

Not long before his retirement, in February 1968, Manley had been elected at the annual conference of the party for the 29th time. A year later, at the 30th annual conference of the PNP, a new leader would be chosen. It was felt at the time of the retirement celebration that the candidate would be Vivian Blake, a young lawyer and Queen's Counsel following very much in the footsteps of the senior Manley. History would prove otherwise.

Manley had considered resigning as party leader as far back as the early 1960s. But on May 31, 1960, when Chief Minister William Alexander Bustamante, a first cousin of Manley's, announced his party's opposition to federation as a matter of policy and declared the JLP's withdrawal from the federal by-election in St Thomas, Manley responded swiftly. Within two weeks he announced his government's intention to call a referendum to decide whether Jamaica should remain in the federation. The Opposition had thrown down the gauntlet, and Manley was a man who could not ignore a challenge. Bustamante's announcement created a fundamental shift in the politics of the country.

Manley believed that the destiny of the West Indies as a nation would be determined by the outcome of this referendum. The JLP had been playing games, and now it was time for those games to end. This was an issue above party politics. Within the ranks of both the party and the Manley family there was initial disbelief and then growing anxiety about holding a referendum. They felt that the party would not survive a vote on a question already sharply dividing the country along partisan political lines. Voters would vote for their parties rather than the issues.

Between 1955 and his loss of the referendum in April 1962, Manley had dominated the political life of Jamaica as leader of a government that could boast a record of integrity, administrative vitality and impressive economic and social achievements. The party had worked long and hard, and now needed more time to put in place its policies and programmes. How could voters in a referendum, even the best educated, answer this paramount federal question if they did not understand the issues? But Manley was obstinate. He was a democrat, and accustomed to struggling with his cousin and rival, Bustamante. The people must decide — that was what democracy was about.

The atmosphere within the party at the time of the announcement of the referendum was therefore not a united one and, to a large extent, Manley stood alone on the issue. If he lost, it was clear he would have to call early elections and, beyond that, consider the legitimacy of his own leadership. The party saw this clearly and believed that the calling of a referendum was therefore a huge mistake, the possible loss of which the party might not survive.

The referendum went ahead in September 1961, and the PNP lost narrowly. Those who knew Manley felt that he never recovered from this blow. Certainly he took full responsibility for the outcome. He also saw the loss in personal terms, questioning himself, his understanding of the people, his decision-making capacities and his leadership. The final insult came when, after calling general elections within months of the referendum, his party was again defeated. It was ironic and deeply hurtful to Manley that it would fall to the Jamaica Labour Party — a party that had never taken independence seriously within or outside a federation — to lead the country into independence in 1962.

By 1969, the PNP having been defeated again in 1967, Norman Manley had witnessed the JLP in office for seven years. It was time for him to retire.

The combined birthday-farewell banquet was put on by the party, and Ivy Ralph, a well-known PNP supporter and fashion designer, was asked to stage a fashion show in Manley's honour after dinner. I was 27 years old at the time, still working at JBC and doing acting and voice-overs and modelling, and Ivy called to ask me to take part. I explained that I had a leading role in the play *Black Comedy* and that it would not be possible for me to attend the function. The play was being staged in a lecture hall at the university by the National Theatre Trust, directed by Lloyd Reckord, one of Jamaica's foremost directors and playwrights. (It was an unusual play that opened in the dark with actors literally feeling their way around. Six years later, as First Lady, I would be an undergraduate student in that same lecture room.) I knew that by the time I left the university that night, it would be too late. She called back to say that she had arranged for the fashion show to begin as late as possible so that I could be there, and that she would wait for me.

As soon as the curtain came down that evening, I rushed out, avoiding well-wishers who would come backstage, jumped into my blue Honda Accord and sped to the National Arena. I was eager to see Norman Manley. I had grown up with an image of him as seen through my father's eyes, as the supreme role model. On my way to the arena I remembered all the things my father had told me about him. Now Jamaican politics would proceed without Manley — it was incomprehensible. I remembered, too, that at one of those meetings my father had had the opportunity to shake Manley's hand. I still recall when Daddy introduced me to him. I was ten, and it was a very special moment in my young life.

When I arrived at the arena, even later than expected, Norman had already delivered his farewell speech; the serious part of the programme had come to an end and the fashion show had not begun. Dinner was over and there was, in the room, a buzz of happiness commingled with sadness: the great man of the PNP was about to leave the political stage. Echoing in the ears of the crowd were the words of Manley paraphrasing the Caribbean-Algerian Franz Fanon, who had written in *The Wretched of the Earth* that 'Every generation has a mission to perform, when one generation sees its own mission let it beware lest it deny the mission of the generation that went before.' This quotation would become embedded in the consciousness of the PNP and would later appear often under a photograph of Michael and his father hugging each other as the mantle passed from the one to the other.

For models, backstage is always fascinating, the atmosphere frantic, with everyone cooperating to help the other get dressed and put on make-up, sharing accessories. It was particularly nerve-racking for me that night, arriving when the others were already dressed in their first outfits and waiting to go on. We didn't have much space and there were clothes on hangers as well as on chairs and on the floor, and I concentrated on quickly getting dressed. We were all excited about modelling with Manley in the audience. When I was finally ready I took a deep breath and plunged out and onto the stage. Once I saw the crowd, all my nervousness disappeared and, as when I was acting in a play, I became someone else — a performer. Memories of past performances before family and friends flashed before me, once again giving me that feeling of being in control. There were many twists and turns to modelling and I knew them all. I strutted and posed, enjoying the appreciation from the crowd.

While on stage, I was aware that most of the spectators were seated at tables scattered around the room, with Norman and Edna Manley and the other dignitaries seated at a head table, looking formal and not really relaxed, and perhaps anxious for it all to be over. As I modelled, I wondered what life must be like for public figures beyond the politics. Then I noticed a group of people not seated at tables, enjoying themselves at the bar — and obviously feeling no pain.

When I returned backstage between wardrobe changes, Ivy asked me to incorporate a little surprise into the modelling programme. I was to leave the stage and dress NW into a dashiki. The dashiki was one of the garments that Ivy and others had popularised in Jamaica. As confident as I was by that time, I thought the stunt was a bad idea. Norman Manley was always very formal in his attire and this evening was no exception; such a stunt would be as embarrassing for him as it would be for me and probably for his wife Edna. Here was a man whom I regarded with awe. I was even a little afraid of him. Someone else would have to carry out the stunt.

But for some reason, Ivy insisted. I peeped through the curtains and realised that Norman Manley's son Michael was one of the people at the bar. Perhaps the thing to do was not to place it on NW, I said, but on his son. Ivy didn't have much time to think about my suggestion, so she just shrugged and went along with the idea. Forty-four-year-old Michael was known as 'Young Boy' — he was at the time a journalist, trade unionist and playboy. Why I thought of putting the dashiki on him I shall never know.

I dressed in a dashiki top, similar to the one I would place on him, and worn as a mini-dress. I hid the other behind me as I sashayed towards Michael, who was leaning on the bar, drink in hand and obviously having a great time. As I made a detour from the route set out for the models, he must have realised something was up. The closer I got to him, the more nervous and uneasy he appeared, shifting from one leg to the other. I felt the entire room focus on the two of us. He started to glance around him with a quizzical look, clearly wondering whether I was really headed for him. Suddenly I was in his face, looking into his eyes. He stuttered, 'Jesus Christ, what the hell is going on?' I was very calm, teasing him as I replied that I didn't intend to put him in any danger. I only wanted to put the dashiki on him.

I was having a wonderful time flirting with this handsome, older man. He begged me not to do whatever it was I was planning to do. I assured him that it would be okay but that first he had to allow me to take off his shirt, which was short-sleeved with buttons down the front. I unbuttoned these one by one, watching his resistance crumble. Now he was up for playing the game. The room's attention was on us. If Ivy wanted drama, she was getting drama. Michael Manley was beginning to revel in the limelight. All the time I was taking his shirt off, I kept talking to him and reassuring him, looking straight into his eyes. But when I pulled the shirt out of his pants something happened to me. I was looking at his body for the first time, his torso long, lean and inviting. For a moment I was overcome, and then I pulled myself together, placed the dashiki on him, completed a full model turn and literally ran off the stage, all to loud applause.

There was a flurry of chitchat afterwards — everyone commenting on how gorgeous Michael Manley was and what a moment it had been. It was as if the transition had already taken place; suddenly NW was forgotten and the new excitement, definitely for those of us backstage, was Michael. No doubt that incident stayed with Michael, too, but what would also remain with him were the prophetic words his father had spoken before I arrived. Addressing his party members, he had explained that he had begun to think seriously of retirement after Bustamante's retirement, due to ill health, two years earlier:

> Pray for this new leader, whoever he may be that he may have the strength and the wisdom to preserve the unity of the party and to give it a new dynamic and a new sense of purpose. I pray that he may receive the support and loyalty in his leadership that he will need if we are to win through, and the political future is to be preserved. I pray for him on the lonely road he must travel, and he will find on his desk so often the legend 'the buck stops here'. So often he will know — if he is a man of deeds and not words — that on his shoulders and his alone rests the finality of decision and action and the judgement of history. I pray that he will, as Antaeus of old, draw strength from the earth, from the courage of the people, the feel of their hands and the sound of their feet, the roar in their throats, and the love of their hearts.

As he stood by the bar having a good time that night, Michael could not have known that his father, unwittingly, was alluding to him. Later, Michael would look back at those words seriously as he experienced both the exhilaration and angst of leadership.

Michael had been single for just a year at the time of his father's retirement, his third wife, Barbara, having died of cancer two years earlier. But he didn't waste any time. He asked me to go out on a date with him later that night. My answer was a firm *no*. Strangely, Michael's eldest daughter Rachel, who was six years younger than me and whom I had met while we were both modelling, had thought that Michael and I should get together. She always appeared to be on the lookout for a wife for her father, and apparently she saw me as a candidate. She kept trying to get us to meet — 'to have tea', as she would put it — but as far as I was concerned, Michael Manley was out of bounds. After that night, Michael continued to try to get me to go out with him on dates, still without success. He must have considered me a challenging project. He did his research, found out what I did, what I liked, who influenced me, anything that would help him to pursue me. What a job he did! He sent me yellow roses, my favourite, twice a day; he got Ivy Ralph to call to implore me to give him my telephone number; he telephoned my office and charmed my secretary, so that she encouraged me to at least return his phone calls. I did not.

I had grown up with a father who was constantly unfaithful with his sweethearts and who had a penchant for frequenting rum bars. I knew Michael's reputation: dating him was out of the question. I was also aware that he was not in my social class. My father's words kept returning to me: stay within your group and be the best you can be in that group. I never saw Michael at any of the social functions I attended. These included fashion shows, dinner parties, and other events among my peers, artists, media professionals and theatre colleagues. I glimpsed him sometimes at National Dance Theatre Company openings and I had heard that during his marriage to Thelma Verity, his second wife, a dancer, he had been involved in an affair with a lead dancer. I couldn't understand why a man like him — probably the most eligible bachelor in Jamaica — would be interested in me, even for a one-night stand. Then there was his family. His mother and father. Norman Manley was the 'Father of the Nation' and his wife, Edna, the 'Mother of the Nation'. NW was someone I worshipped from afar. He was definitely not the type of person with whom I could imagine sitting down to dinner. Michael's elder brother and only sibling, Douglas, was another matter; the few times I saw him, he appeared to be totally wrapped up in himself, like an eccentric professor. I remember first seeing him in my late teens, when I worked for Perry Henzell. I would watch him walking down Duke Street dressed casually in sandals. I had a quiet crush on him. He was cute, I thought, but off limits because he was of another generation.

When Michael started asking me out, I had just finished a long-term relationship so I was not in a hurry to get involved again. I was looking for neither commitment nor marriage. Before this, I had dated mainly white men who were in Jamaica working in the advertising industry or doing consultancies of one kind or another. My mother had socialised me not to have sex until I was married.

I hardly had time for a serious relationship anyway. I was leading a celebrity life at JBC both on radio and television. I had numerous social activities apart from the station, many of them involving my flatmate Audrey. A graduate in Literature from Boston University, Audrey was about ten years older than I was. She was expanding my world, and relentlessly teaching me how to be an excellent broadcaster. She watched and listened to as many of my radio and television programmes as possible and gave me honest, often unflattering, feedback. Later, when she was a senior television producer for the Jamaica Information Service (JIS) — the government broadcasting service — she would use me to anchor JIS programmes. This often involved going into rural Jamaica to do interviews, returning to the studio and presenting the broadcast. Audrey and I supported each other. Life was great.

By now I was in my late twenties and economically independent. I received a good salary from JBC, but the majority of my earnings came from voicing commercials and documentaries for both radio and television. I had a strong belief, which came from my mother's example and lecturettes, that I should not be financially dependent on any man.

When Audrey announced not only that she was getting married but that she would be leaving the country to live in Canada, I took the opportunity to assess my life. I decided to fulfill my dream to study. My sister Shirley had gone to university, and for a long time I had wanted to go myself. Audrey invited me to join her in Canada and enroll in Ryerson Polytechnical College in Toronto, which was and is well known for its broadcasting programme.

As it turned out, I would not attend Ryerson and it would be some years before I would go to university. But as I observed how happy Audrey was with her fiancé, I began to develop a yearning for commitment. The stage was set.

I finally gave in to Michael Manley and agreed to a single date. This was within months of his election as party leader and about a year after meeting him at the National Arena. By this time I was wary of men, particularly those who came with promises of love. I didn't expect the relationship to work, and in part that was why I finally agreed to see him — to prove that to myself and to him.

We agreed that since we were both public persons, we would at first meet in secret. This was important, he said, because as leader of the Opposition he was determined to take his party to victory in the 1972 elections and he did not want to upset the applecart. We had to avoid doing anything that might be perceived as even slightly controversial. He was bothered by his playboy image, by the fact that he had been married three times. His other reality was that he was a near-white Jamaican. He used to say that if there was anything he could do to become black, like the majority of Jamaicans, he would. I would reply that the masses of people saw him as black and referred to him as black. But this never sufficed — he wanted to be a black man more than anything else in the world. To me it seemed that the different backgrounds from which we came — the colour and class issue — hovered over us. So although I had been socialised into marrying a high-brown man, I was confronting for the first time these issues of colour, status and class. And there was lingering doubt — why me? Nevertheless, we began dating.

There was hostility from some quarters, curiosity from others, and openness among a limited few in his social circle who either accepted me easily or were persuaded by him to do so. In spite of the decision to hide, we often went to private dinner parties hosted by his close friends. We also spent time with other couples on weekends: Barclay and Glynne Ewart,

Douglas and Sheila Graham, O.K. and Angela Melhado, and John and Valerie Marzouca — all from his social class. Michael was always supportive and protective of me at these gatherings.

As we got to know each other, to take increasing delight in each other; Michael taught me how the other half of Jamaica lived and I did the same for him. We discussed how both 'halves' existed, separate but intertwined. He shared with me his passion for justice in the broadest sense of the term. From early on we recognised that ours would be a dynamic, personal, public and political relationship — one that far exceeded the bounds of 'being in love'.

I recall the night he took me to a small dinner party being given by his close friends, Ken and Valerie McNeill. Ken was a highly regarded ENT specialist. I was both curious and anxious about this dinner party. I didn't want to embarrass Michael or let him down. This was one of the first times that his friends would be aware of our relationship. I expressed my fears to him beforehand, and he reassured me that everything would be fine. He told me to just keep my eyes on him. He would sit opposite me.

Drinks before dinner went well and I began to relax a little. Then we sat down to dinner. For the first course they served escargots in the shell. When the dish was placed before me I didn't know what it was and didn't like the way it looked. Then I saw the strange-looking cutlery that I was supposed to use to get the escargots into my mouth and I really panicked. Cold sweat crept over me and I wanted to run away. What on earth was I doing here? I did not belong. Only Michael's encouraging eyes from across the table prevented me from getting up and running straight out the house and out of his life.

I watched him as he slowly picked up an escargot with the odd cutlery. I followed suit. But with my best efforts, as I tentatively attempted to squeeze the odd apparatus and grasp the escargot with its tentacles, the escargot slipped out. I had been so convinced that I had it where I wanted it, that I was surprised when it took off on a journey of its own — it simply took flight, ending up across the table and on the ground. I had never been more embarrassed in my life. But my hosts would not have their guest feel awkward in any way. They proceeded as if nothing untoward had happened. I was now more determined more than ever to control the escargot. My competitive self took over, and I made it through the rest of the meal without incident.

After dinner, when we were driving home, Michael and I laughed about the escargot. I loved his chuckle, with its promise of a guffaw. It was okay after all. I had not let him down. He told me that I was a real trooper and that he admired the way I had carried on despite the initial slip. I knew then that I was falling in love with him.

Escargots were just one of many foods from this other world that I would learn to eat and enjoy. There were, for example, cow's tongue, which eventually would become a weekly staple in our home, veal, and steak tartar. In time I developed a taste for all these foods.

I had no difficulty over Michael's wish for secrecy. I didn't want my circle of friends to know that I was dating this older man either. I had mentioned to some of them that I was thinking of going out with him and the response was, 'You're crazy.' Not only was he an aging playboy, they said, but worst of all, he was a politician. My friends also felt that I was way out of my league and that the relationship just could not work. How did I plan to handle his mother and the rest of his family? they asked. Perhaps these doubters made me all the more determined that the relationship should succeed. No matter what Michael's schedule, we saw each other every day — sometimes more than once. In the early days of the courtship, hiding proved to be problematic because I was by then a public figure myself. So here we were hiding and at the same time unable to stay away from each other.

Michael was a marrying kind of man. His first wife was a white French woman, Jacqueline Kamellard, 12 years his senior. Michael was a 22-year-old student at the London School of Economics when they married there in 1946. Jacqueline's previous marriage had been to a Jamaican, Robert Verity, and had produced two children, Jeremy and Anita. At the time of this marriage, Michael was involved in activism through the West Indian Students Union and in particular through the campaign for the Referendum on the West Indies Federation. During his London years, both as a student and as a journalist for the BBC, he corresponded with his parents on a regular basis. These letters were largely about British and world politics and about the horrors of communism. Whatever the content of the letters, he always managed to put in a plea for money, living, as he was, as a married student with a ready-made family.

One year after he and Jacqueline married, they had a daughter, Rachel. The marriage lasted five years, and Rachel was just three years old at the time of the break-up. She was sent to live with her grandparents, Norman and Edna Manley, in Jamaica. Later that year Michael himself returned to Jamaica, but Rachel continued to live with her grandparents. By the age of 27, Michael had experienced his first serious heartbreak and divorce.

His second marriage took place four years after the end of the first. This time he wed in Jamaica, to Thelma Verity, a Jamaican of Afro-Chinese ancestry and a dancer. To complicate matters, Thelma's adoptive parents were the family of Robert Verity, Jacqueline's first husband and a close friend of Norman Manley's. This marriage also produced one child, Joseph, born in 1958, almost 11 years after the arrival of Rachel. The context for this second marriage was again Michael's activism, this time in Jamaica, in part through his career as a journalist at the now defunct weekly nationalist newspaper, the *Public Opinion*. He was also involved in building the National Workers Union after the split within the PNP, which resulted in the virtual demise of the left-wing Trade Union Congress under the communist Ken Hill. The four Hs, as they were known, Ken Hill, his brother Frank Hill, Arthur Henry and Richard Hart, were expelled from the party in 1952. In his *Public Opinion* column titled 'The Root of the Matter', Michael wrote about his support for his father's decision to expel the left wing. The tension between politics and family life continued to plague him. Michael's second marriage, like his first, lasted five years.

Six years later Michael married Barbara Lewars-Carter, a woman of Indian extraction and easily the most beautiful woman I had ever seen. I had met her while we were both appearing in a television commercial for Red Stripe Beer. I remember she appeared shy, but was in fact very friendly. This would have been just before she began to date Michael.

Tragically, Barbara died of cancer soon after their marriage. The tumour was discovered during the birth in 1967 of their only child, Sarah. Within days she was diagnosed with meningitis, but fortunately recovered from it. Barbara's death turned Michael's life upside down again. It was during his marriage to her that the idea of his becoming leader of the party first surfaced. A group of friends supported by Barbara had set out to convince him that this was possible. By that time he had already been a senator and had also become the member of parliament for East Central Kingston, having won by a historically narrow margin in a last-minute run for the seemingly unwinnable JLP seat.

When I met him in 1969, Michael was still mourning Barbara's death and was being encouraged vigorously by her mother, Gloria Lewars, to take gifts to the grave on Barbara's birthday as well as to continue conversations with John Hoad, a Methodist parson who had ministered to her while she was dying. Gloria and Barbara's sister, Marguerite, would be among those who resisted my marriage to Michael. I, however, was too smitten to care.

When I was introduced through Michael to Jamaican political life in late 1969, I didn't have a clue what my role would turn out to be. I knew only that I was suddenly in a position of influence. While I got to know Michael personally I was also able to observe his political side. Leadership took enormous commitment and discipline: going on the road day after day, listening to people as they told us long stories about their lives, each one involving some problem which demanded immediate attention. The support of the comrades around us was invaluable as we sought to meet the needs of the people in any way we could. In Michael I saw someone who was hard-working and a perfectionist. In all my experience in public life, the only leader who came even close to him in terms of charisma and ability to 'play' an audience was Fidel Castro.

Michael was very class-conscious, and although his life's work was for the masses, he knew little or nothing about them at an individual level and was uncomfortable around them. I think that they sensed his discomfort and, as a result, often communicated with him through me. They would say to me, 'Sister Bev — take a message to Michael.' Relaying such messages became one of the many tasks I would perform for him.

Michael grew up with a mother who was unusually independent for her time. As an artist, Edna led a life surrounded by other artists who often met socially, not only inside, but away from Drumblair. She talked about making herself anonymous by wearing wigs and going to Port Royal to put her feet in the water, often accompanied by a male artist. Michael had a love–hate relationship with his mother and perhaps he translated this into love–hate relationships with all his women. He once told me how, as a little boy, he loved lying in his bed and waiting for his mother to come in and say good-night. Often she would be on her way out with his father on some social occasion, and she would twirl her wide skirts and crinolines for Michael. He told me that as he grew up, he sometimes felt in love with his mother and jealous of his father.

He told me of one evening when he had worked himself into a jealous rage and decided he would attack his father. He stood, a baseball bat in his hand, behind the door that NW opened. But that evening NW came in through another door and saw Michael, bat in hand. He asked him what on earth he was doing. Michael remembered mumbling something and walking away, embarrassed. Would he have hit his father? Even Michael didn't know.

The other women he would have observed while he was growing up were also strong women. They included his father's two sisters, Michael's aunts Vera and Muriel. Vera was an accomplished musician and Muriel was a pediatrician. Vera married Dr Ludlow Moody, a medical doctor, while Muriel remained a spinster. Both were highly independent women. The other women in his life were those who worked in his parents' household — the housekeeper 'Miss B' and the cook, Zethilda.

As an adult, Michael was like a magnet to women. They adored him and he adored them. He delighted in giving all the women in his life anything they wanted that it was in his power to provide. His wives were singled out for extra special treatment, perhaps because they were the mothers of his children and the ones who kept the home environment safe and secure. He knew how to make women feel special, cared for and protected. For him it was something of an art form. He was obsessive about women and he knew it. He always got what he wanted.

One thing that was problematic for me was the narrowness of the group of friends upon whom Michael depended for many reasons, including funding for the PNP and leading projects at the national and constituency level. Some of these friends even ran for office. We were always in the company of married couples with whom I felt unable to compete — economically or socially.

We spent weekends together; we spent summer holidays together every year. There seemed to me to be too few boundaries there. They understood and lived the life of the upper class. The wives had special clothes for every occasion; their husbands were wealthy businessmen.

Michael, on the other hand, never had money. When I first met him, he lived off a union salary supplemented by a bank overdraft. His residence was a small two-bedroom apartment. To me it seemed pathetic the way he lived, but it didn't seem to matter to him. Money to Michael was something you used when you had it. He spent money on very specific things — his music, his car, his clothes and his art — and he was a terrible money manager.

Beginning a relationship with Michael Manley, I willingly walked into a situation of guilt and confusion with ex-wives and children from three previous marriages. In addition, Michael was unsure of himself as a father. Observing Michael's family, it seemed to me that they were all from another world. How could someone have a child with each of three wives, and not maintain a relationship with them except on a formal basis — having breakfast or dinner with each one once a week, as carefully noted in his diary? He paid attention to his family, but with a kind of military precision. I didn't get it. I knew about absentee fathers, largely in the working class, but this was something different — this detached fathering. Michael assured me that I would not have to mother any of his other children and that my contact with them would be minimal and relegated to short visits. At the time, I was happy for this reassurance because the thought of mothering in such circumstances made me anxious. I already knew Rachel, of course, but not as a stepmother. Soon, however, I took an interest in his children and began to recognise the importance of parents communicating with each other, particularly after a marital break-up. The children were all very different, but as I got to know each one, I developed a deep and abiding love for them.

By 1969 Michael's daughter Rachel was a grown woman. Michael was never quite sure what she was up to, even when she was only a girl. Occasionally, she would telephone from wherever she was in the world. But for him, in those days, Rachel — whom we called Ra — always spelled trouble. They fought constantly; she was a rebellious teenager and did not take kindly to his relationships. She admitted to having played a role in destroying Michael's second and third marriages. Each time he married, Michael had taken Ra from her paternal grandparents, Norman and Edna, and brought her to live with him and his new wife, but although they each desperately wanted to nurture a father–daughter relationship, neither knew how. I often wondered what it was like for Ra, who, during the course of her young life, had been shuttled from her grandparents' place to a new home each time her father remarried. She wanted to have a relationship with her father, while he was busy falling in love with other women. No wonder she stayed out of Jamaica for long periods of time. In spite of her traumatic life, however, she has managed to maintain an innocent, childlike quality interlaced with mischief and to develop a quick and probing mind.

As for Joseph, or Jo as we called him, Michael had a stormy relationship with his mother, his second wife, Thelma. Michael was always uptight with Thelma and couldn't seem to converse with her without quarrelling. He had breakfast with Jo once a week; this was always put in his diary so that he wouldn't forget. He never liked these breakfasts because Thelma was there and the atmosphere was often tense and contrived. He had to discipline himself to go. I doubt it was an ideal environment in which to bond with his son. I was never invited to breakfast, and I was always particularly careful when Jo visited. Michael warned me that Thelma was the kind of person who would ask Jo questions about me on his return home, and it was important that we not add any fuel to her fire. I gave Jo as much love as I could. I remember him as being shy during his growing up — the fact that he had a stammer didn't help — but with an extraordinary mind for detail. Michael always regretted that Jo was not interested in sports, as this would have been a wonderful way for them to connect. They tried playing football while he was still married to Thelma, but it didn't work because Jo was no athlete. He was such a little intellectual, but also a boy who wanted very much to please his parents.

Michael had dinner with his daughter Sarah and her maternal grandparents once a week at Cooper's Hill, where they lived. Grandfather Russell Lewars was a former town clerk of the municipality of Kingston and St Andrew, and he was a lovely, unassuming man. His wife Gloria had an austere, domineering and controlling personality. At first she did not approve of me, at least not as the person Michael would marry after her daughter Barbara. Although Michael had a cordial relationship with them, he did not enjoy those dinners, for he felt they were more about maintaining a relationship with

Russell and Gloria than getting to know Sarah. She would have supper with them and then, like clockwork, be sent off to bed, while he had to remain and chat with the grandparents.

Michael never talked to Sarah about her mother, Barbara, even when she was old enough to have such discussions. Occasionally, he would pick her up and take her out for drives, but, although he tried, he had great difficulty relaxing enough to talk to her about anything personal. I encouraged him to exercise his rights as a father and have Sarah visit him in his own home, but at first Sarah's grandparents were adamant and refused to allow this. Gloria overprotected Sarah and wouldn't let her visit our home because she feared that we were not capable of taking care of her. When Michael insisted that the time had come for her to visit overnight — she must have been five years old — she arrived with a carefully packed suitcase and a long list of instructions and medication for every possible type of illness. There was also a list of the clothing in the suitcase. After much persistence her grandparents relented and Sarah began to visit on a regular basis. When this happened I had to become a mother overnight.

Sarah and I bonded quickly and I soon began to look forward to her visits. I remember her as loving and warm and willing to open up to a friendship with me. We listened to musicals together, including *The Sound of Music,* which was our special record. I made sure that what she experienced with us was neither contrived nor controlling. I was determined to prove to her grandmother that Michael and I could take care of her and that, although I wasn't Barbara, I was good enough for Michael. This was very important to me because Gloria Lewars was the kind of upper middle-class woman who represented everything that was intimidating to me. Whenever I was in her presence, which was not often because Michael was not allowed to take me to her home when he visited Sarah, I felt that she was judging me. I didn't compare to Barbara, who was recognised by everyone in Jamaica as beautiful and talented. Once again, as in my childhood, I felt like the odd one out.

Not surprisingly, Michael's former wives and children dominated a great deal of our early conversations. Michael carried an enormous burden of guilt over his children. I don't think he ever forgave himself for the fact that he went against Barbara's dying wish that her mother should not bring up Sarah. But Michael just didn't see how he could keep Sarah at the time, and Gloria Lewars was the kind of person who took charge. He also felt a great deal of guilt about Rachel. His marriage to Jacqueline had ended so quickly and suddenly he found himself with this little girl. He was young and barely out of university, he did what he thought was best for her and sent her to Jamaica to his parents. The memory of this little girl making the long trip alone from London to Jamaica to live with grandparents she was meeting for the first time haunted him all his life. Why had he given her away? Had it been the best thing for her? He had only been doing what he felt he had to do, but now could he ever really fit into her life? Later, when Rachel became rebellious, he felt responsible. Eventually he just stayed away from her as much as possible, hoping things would sort themselves out.

As for me, I just couldn't understand how a father could have this type of relationship with his children, supporting them exactly as the court decided, on a monthly basis and no more, and not developing good relations with his ex-wives. Ra's mother lived in England, and although Michael visited that country from time to time, he never contacted her. When I met him, he was still bitter about her and blamed her for his first heartache. He was also angry with Thelma, and he was still grieving over Barbara.

Michael and I eventually moved in together, and lived in a rented place for nearly three years. With Michael having been married three times already, we didn't want to do anything to reinforce his playboy image, to 'rock the boat' with the electorate. The thought of wife number four was too much. I understood this. In the tiny two-bedroom flat in which he lived when I had first met him, one of those rooms was very small and he used it as a study. His previous girlfriend had done a wonderful job of decorating the place. It was what he could afford on a meagre union salary. When Joseph came to visit he would sleep in the study. During his time at this flat, Rachel was abroad, and Sarah never visited.

Our lifestyle centred mostly on politics, and more and more we were on the road campaigning. The flat was often filled with comrades and various people who were there to discuss political issues, particularly how these would be formulated into policy and implemented, if and when Michael came to office. Various groups and task forces consulted with him on a regular basis on such matters as health and education, and he even appointed a shadow cabinet.

Soon the small flat had outlived its usefulness and we began to shop around for something larger. Michael suggested that we move into the house he had built for Thelma and where he had also lived with Barbara, who had died there. When NW sold Drumblair, he kept a lot for himself, where he built his house, gave Michael a lot, and kept one for his sister Muriel. Michael's house, Ebony Hill, was rented at the time that we were thinking of moving, and it was his intention that we should move in when the lease was up. But I was firm. I told him I didn't want to live, even temporarily, in a house that still held memories of two of his ex-wives. There seemed too much past unhappiness there.

Instead we moved to a rented three-bedroom, two-bathroom house on Garth Road. We used one of the bedrooms as an office for Michael. We installed a door into the garden from the study so that our many visitors could come and go without walking through the house.

Meanwhile, our relationship was deepening, and eventually it progressed to the stage that one day Michael told me it was time for me to be 'officially' introduced to Edna Manley as his girlfriend. I was terrified. The girl from the flat above the railroad station was about to dine with the 'Mother of the Nation'.

Chapter 5

I had met Edna Manley once before, briefly, when Norman lay dying. During the days before his death in September 1969, I had been in their home, had watched his still beautiful bronze body prostrate in a hospital bed that had been brought there. As he drifted in and out of consciousness, Edna entered and left her husband's room in a daze, walking briskly and lightly as she was wont to do, an anxious, fleeting apparition.

The night before he died, it became my job to drive Aunt Mu to the airport to meet Rachel, who was arriving from The Bahamas, unaware that her Pardi was dying. During the drive there, we kept up a forced merry chatter, largely focusing on what would become of Edna after NW, or Pardi, died. To this day one of my regrets is that because NW was so ill and reclusive the year that Michael and I started dating, I never got to know him. Months before his death, he had literally resigned from life. These were challenging times for the Manley family, and Michael became closer to his mother as she watched her only love, her Norman, ebb away from her.

They had met when Norman went to England as a Rhodes Scholar. By then Norman's siblings, Vera, Muriel and Roy, were already living in England. On a visit to his maternal aunt, Ellie Swithenbank, in Penzance, England, Norman first got to know Edna. By the time they next met, they were already falling desperately in love. They corresponded while Norman was away at war — he ended up on the front in France — and married in 1921. Michael told me that it was an instance of opposites attracting: Norman was stern and disciplined and Edna was considered a 'wild card'. In addition, she was fiercely dedicated to her art and could not see herself in a committed relationship. While Edna was certain about what she wanted to do in terms of her sculpture, NW was unsure of his future and was still searching for something meaningful to do.

Over the years, Edna had grown accustomed to meeting Michael's girlfriends. She took his attachments in her stride and became involved only with the serious ones, often aiding and abetting him when he needed an accomplice. She had a cottage in the Blue Mountains, and would lend him a key, knowing he was taking some woman there.

My reaction to Michael's suggestion that she and I meet 'officially', which came about a year after we starting seeing each other, was that it was too early. I was nervous at the thought, but Michael wanted her approval, and felt that our meeting formally would make family gatherings more comfortable. I had seen Edna in public over the years, of course; she often accompanied her husband to political rallies, but she never spoke. When she was acknowledged as his wife, she waved. She was present, but I always had the feeling that it was as a duty, that she was absent emotionally.

By now I had started touring the country with Michael, but I usually remained hidden in the car. I was growing accustomed to hiding, and felt I wasn't ready to come out of hiding to meet his mother, his brother Douglas, and his father's sister Muriel, known as Auntie Mu. I was even more scared of Auntie Mu than I was of Edna; she was a tiny, formidable woman from the 'old school', and I knew I had to be perfect for her. But Michael was insistent. He would not allow me to put off the visit. He felt that fear was something you did not run away from. There was what he referred to as big 'fraid' and little 'fraid' and he said it was important always to be bigger than your fear.

It didn't help that the meeting with his mother was to take place over lunch, which I have always felt is the most abstract of meals. I just prayed there would be no embarrassments like the flying escargots. As we entered the driveway I noticed, as I had the first time I'd been there, that the name of the house was Regardless. It was Michael's daughter Rachel's idea; she had named the house after seeing the British comedy film *Carry On Regardless*. At the time, the family was dealing with the loss of the first general elections following independence. Mardi loved the name.

It was a typical Jamaican day, the sky blue and with hardly a cloud. The gate was wide open. The driveway curved river-like up a slight grade from the house, which, though it stood on a mound, was discreetly hidden from view. Privacy was very important to the Manleys, for they had lived under the public eye so long. My first impression was that the house was relatively simple, almost austere. Michael owned the house next door, named Ebony Hill because of the beautiful ebony trees growing around it, and there was a connecting gate between the two homes. Both Thelma and Barbara had lived at Ebony Hill during their marriages to Michael, although it had been built for

Thelma. Joseph and Sarah were born there, and Rachel had lived there at various times over the years.

The front doors of the house slid open wide and, as we walked through them, I heard the sound of dogs. I have always been terrified of dogs, but Edna loved them and had always had them. They were not just pets but guard dogs, sleek ,black Doberman pinschers. Michael explained that they were well trained, intelligent dogs and an intruder's worst nightmare. It was not unknown, he said, for this kind of dog to keep an intruder trapped in one place for a long period of time, and attack if the intruder moved. Edna lived alone in this house that she and Norman built after they had sold the Drumblair lands to pay his political debts. She was lonely and sad over losing her husband, but she stubbornly carried on, living alone in the house with her cook, Zethilda, and her gardener, Batiste.

That day we passed through a long, wide room and down a long hallway to the patio at the back, where three years later Michael would take me as his bride. I noticed the table set in a separate dining room to the left; crystal, china and starched white placemats and napkins caught my eye. I also saw, on a mahogany sideboard, a bell, which surprised me because comrades hardly ever used a bell. It was the JLP symbol. This bell, I would learn, remained on the sideboard except at mealtime, when Edna would keep it beside her on the table. The dining room was small and intimate and dominated by a round antique table. The table could seat six comfortably which, in the Drumblair days might stretch to two dozen with the addition of all its leaves. I was impressed by the fact that Zethilda, the cook who had served the Manley household for decades, wore a stiffly starched white apron and cap. She was short and black, and she had about her a long-suffering air. She looked at me with a face that seemed to express both empathy and curiosity as to why I was there. I suppose she had seen other girlfriends and wives come and go. 'Mr Michael' was up to it again. She also had an idea of the toll that Mr Michael's philandering had taken on his mother, her employer. I got the impression that hers was not a face that smiled often, but when Michael greeted her, she smiled for him.

The patio looked out on a lovely, well-kept garden, which included a night-blooming Cereus as well as orchids and hibiscus. I could see immediately where Michael had learned his love of nature. There on the patio was where Edna entertained her friends. Just below it was a small cottage that Roy, her grandson, later occupied. Beside the house and to the left of the patio was Edna's studio, where she did her sculpting, and on the other side, Auntie Mu's cottage, which lay at the bottom of the Ebony Hill garden. This one-bedroom cottage was to become Michael's on Auntie Mu's death. The three homes — Regardless, Ebony Hill, and Auntie Mu's cottage — made up the Manley compound, with which I was to become quite familiar.

No one else was present — just Edna, Michael and myself. Michael had prepared me for this meeting. And beforehand I had done my research on her art and on her husband's political and legal career, so that I would have something to talk about. Nevertheless, I was uneasy.

Edna Manley was a tall, slim, elegant woman whose presence could not be missed. People often stood up as she entered a room. She moved quickly and effortlessly, always maintaining the perfect posture of a younger woman. One of the first things I recognised about her was her intellect and her grace. She spoke knowledgeably on a range of subjects while always ensuring that I was not left out of the conversation. It was well known that Norman had an enormous intellect, and somehow Edna had managed to disguise her own so that his would appear dominant. Her commitment to Norman Manley was such that she stayed with him even though that meant subordinating her art to his politics. I was aware of this during our first real meeting, and I admired her balancing act.

Michael called Edna 'Mother', in a voice tinged with respect and awe — in something like the clipped tone of the professor in *My Fair Lady*. His relationship with her was complex, and their tension would often lead him to avoid visits, hardly speaking to her for fairly long periods, though he always took care of her needs. He told me that he just couldn't deal with her neuroses and drama all the time. She was prone to making up stories; she had a vivid imagination. And she would throw tantrums if she didn't get her own way. Yet even in her absence, she dominated his life and his decisions. Furthermore, he respected the genius of her art. When she acted up, he would always remind whoever was present about her talent. After his father died, Michael became her number one adviser and critic on all current projects. She consulted him and he loved it. Michael appreciated art and was himself a collector. At one stage in his life, after leaving the London School of Economics — he was there from 1948–51 — he had even thought he might make a living as an art critic.

Michael's brother, Douglas, did not talk to his mother much either. I remember that he kept his orchids in her back garden and it was not unusual for him to arrive, walk by his mother without saying a word to her, check that his orchids were okay, and then walk back through the house and leave. All this appeared so strange to me. The Manley family was very different from the one in which I had grown up. In time this would make me all the more determined to play a role in improving Michael's relationships with ex-wives, children and his mother, and I like to believe that I succeeded somewhat.

That first meeting with Edna began with drinks on the patio before lunch. She was charming and I was fascinated by the way her mind worked. She seemed curious and wanted to know as much about me as possible, yet was careful not to make me uncomfortable with her questions. Michael seemed quite relaxed, which made things easier. I managed to get through lunch without any faux pas and even enjoyed the occasion. The conversation was fascinating. They talked about arts, politics and philosophy, both ensuring that I was always part of the conversation. Mardi was anxious to know more about the JBC and the extent to which it was keeping to its goals of nation building. She also expressed the hope that partisan politics was not interfering with the JBC's operation. And so, in the end that day, all went well. She even asked to see me the following afternoon. Thus began a friendship whose special closeness was to last for many years.

But there were more tests to come. I was then to meet Muriel Manley, an even more intimidating Matriarch of the family. The night of that dinner, Michael and I had drinks with Edna and then all three of us walked down the path to Aunt Muriel's cottage. We entered the small one-bedroom cottage through the kitchen. I held Michael's hand tightly and he squeezed mine, giving me the confidence and courage I needed. Most of the evening was a blur but I do remember being on my best behaviour and doing everything right. Michael's Auntie Mu, Dr Muriel Manley, gave a life of service to the public health sector at the Mary Issa Children's Crèche. She was a short woman, probably not more than four feet tall. She was always conservatively dressed in dark grey clothes and sensible shoes and stockings. She kept her hair tamed in a net with a bun at the back of her head. As tiny as she was, she was a frightening prospect to many, and I felt that I would never meet with her approval. She was proper and stern, and I saw in her what my father thought his daughters would become if no one asked them to marry. She neither acquired wealth nor had any interest in doing so. She lived with a housekeeper, Mae, who was quite insane and who from time to time would have to be hospitalised in a mental institution. We would often hear her from Edna's house ranting and raving. That first night, I expressed no opinions of my own. All Auntie Mu's opinions became mine. Terrified, I wondered what she really thought of me, but that was not the kind of discussion one had with Auntie Mu. Over time I would become less nervous around her.

As Edna and I got to know each other better, we started to do a number of things together, including personal shopping. She always sought my advice on what to wear because she felt that, as she grew older, she no longer knew what was fashionable. After Norman died, the evenings were particularly stressful for her between the hours of 6:00 and 8:00, as that was when Norman would come home. We spent a great deal of that time together, during which she asked me to call her by the name affectionately used by the family, Mardi. Norman and Edna had both agreed that they did not wish to be called Grandpa or Grandma, and after discussion with Rachel, they settled for her suggestion to call them Pardi and Mardi.

Mardi always prefaced our discussions by saying that she didn't like giving advice, and proceeded to give it anyway. From early, she warned me about the ways in which I should and should not 'involve' myself as Michael's wife. Never get involved in the party in any way, she cautioned. Do things that bordered on the innocuous. Involvement in the party, over and beyond kissing babies and cutting ribbons, would only create tension between Michael and me. It would also prevent me from being there for Michael when he needed me, when his heart would surely be broken by politics as his father's had been. I couldn't understand why she was so firm on these issues. Yet even as she was giving me this advice, she was providing me with books to read on women such as Golda Meir and Eleanor Roosevelt — one a prime minister, and the other an activist First Lady who, after her husband died, became a diplomat. I often wondered about the choices Edna, a near-white English woman, had had to make and how she had balanced the role of artist with that of a political leader's wife. Achieving such a balance must have been difficult for her in a country that did not yet understand that women, even wives, had rights.

Mardi also introduced me to authors she liked, in particular novelist Doris Lessing, whose work was based mostly on her own life. She would present the books on significant days in my life, wedding anniversaries and birthdays. She believed these milestones were important and should be celebrated accordingly. Lessing's fiction often addresses the theme of women and their liberation — at one stage *The Golden Notebooks* was actually called *Free Women*. She explores the possibility of women being economically independent even though they might be emotionally dependent on men. *The Golden Notebooks* became one of my favourite works, a reference point for me as a woman, and later for my role as wife of the prime minister.

Mardi spoke to me about the leadership roles that Golda Meir had played before and after she became prime minister of Israel at age 74. Meir had recognised at an early age that what came first for her was to make a difference in the fight on behalf of Jews all over the world for their own homeland. Everything would be sacrificed for that cause, that huge idea. Meir gave up on her marriage when her children were still young. Her husband, Maurice, was a wonderful husband and father but the fight did not come first for him. Throughout her life she would be plagued by guilt over having had to leave her husband and the impact that had on her children. But she did what she had to do.

Mardi's third role model of sorts, Eleanor Roosevelt, she described as 'the intellectual wife' of a US president. Eleanor came from a wealthy family and was therefore economically independent and carved out a place for herself, not only in filling her role as the president's wife, but also in doing her own thing through the speeches she made and her weekly newspaper columns. She was an active First Lady and people regarded her as an individual with the capacity to wield power in her own right. When she became aware of her husband's infidelities, she decided to remain his wife, in name only. She never embarrassed him, but put on a brave face and suffered greatly in private.

The voices of these three women — Lessing, Meir and Roosevelt — would resonate in my head often in the years to come. Mardi became a major influence on my life, not so much by telling me what to do — she hated that — but by introducing me to the stories of these great women who had had such an impact on her own life. They were a priceless gift from her to me.

Mardi always said that she would never become a little old lady ensconced in a shawl and rocking in her chair. Women had to be courageous and strong to their dying day, she told me. She watched me continuously, and told me that she was confident I had the capacity to become such a woman. I listened to her words in awe. This was a new world for me. It would take me months, or even years, to understand what she was saying. I had what appeared to be everything I wanted in life. In those early golden days, I was not aware of the challenges facing me, personal or political, until they were upon me.

Despite her many accomplishments, Mardi did not believe that motherhood was something at which she had been successful. She had not been a 'good' mother, she said, a traditional mother who wanted to spend the major part of her life with her two children. When the boys were young she would take off to the country, to Arthur's Seat in Mandeville, to spend quality time with them and to carve. Norman would join her for part of the time, then leave her with the boys, their nanny and their friends for an extra week or so. George Campbell, the housekeeper's nephew, became a regular part of the holiday group. (He would later become the poet of the 1930s 'revolution'.)

Although I respected Mardi, I felt that some things had changed since her day. I dismissed her warnings about party involvement. There was so much to be done and I was going to take the load off Michael as much as possible. I was a young, black woman in my early thirties and I knew that, if called to give duty to my country through marriage to a prime minister, I could help to bring fundamental changes to Jamaica and, in particular, to the marginalized masses. Black people had to have their say and this had to be manifest in every way — through our culture, including hairstyle and dress, as well as by creating indigenous ways, based on our African heritage, to reach our full potential.

To my amazement, Michael not only understood this but also was able to articulate it like no one else. We often talked about the rigours and horrors of the Middle Passage and the need, as Marcus Garvey had affirmed decades before, to emancipate ourselves from mental slavery as none but ourselves could free our minds. We discussed retracing those steps mentally so that we could recognise Africa as our homeland and, with this understanding, rebuild a Jamaican culture with confidence and pride.

As an artist, Mardi strove to help Jamaicans accept an image of themselves as black and beautiful. This was demonstrated in her early Jamaican carvings, among them *Negro Aroused,* which is still seen as symbolic of the working class struggle for better wages and working conditions. She sent out birthday cards, particularly those to her grandchildren, graced with the faces of African children — which weren't easy to find at the time. Recognising how important it was for blacks to have a positive self-image, she never chose cards with white subjects.

Music was very important to the Manley family. Michael prepared me by giving me my first lessons in classical music in case Mardi invited us to listen to it with her after a meal. She would probably play Mahler, he said. He told me a little about the music of Mahler, adding that it would take some getting used to. He warned me that listening to music in any Manley household was a serious affair and particularly so in his mother's home. I must not talk while the music was being played. Any comments I had should come after. There were certain musical pieces Mardi could not enjoy because she felt they were too depressing; Mahler reminded her of Norman, who had played the composer's music day after day when he was ill. But there were many other pieces of classical music that they had enjoyed together. After Norman died, Michael substituted for his father in many ways; one of them was listening to and appreciating classical music with his mother.

Gradually I developed an understanding of, and appreciation for, classical music as we sat together, listening to every phrase, listening for what was behind the music and hearing the different instruments as they dominated others. We often talked afterwards about the music and the conductor and Michael would seem transported to some far-off place — far from the day-to-day challenges of his political life. Later, on one of our trips to London, Michael would keep his earlier promise and introduce me to the Royal Albert Hall on the river Thames — an extraordinary setting — where we listened to the works of Beethoven. Hearing the music, watching the conductor and the orchestra in that vast arena was a truly awe-inspiring experience.

I remember being acutely aware that day, particularly during the intermission, that mine was the only black face. I wondered whether black people did not come to places like this. It was an uncomfortable feeling, and Michael, without saying anything, obviously knew how I felt. He was completely at ease and at home in this environment, but he never let go of my hand, squeezing it occasionally to reassure me. The woman on his arm was always the only woman in the world at that particular time and it was a great feeling to have what seemed to be his complete attention. By my next visit to the concert hall, I had forgotten those thoughts of race and difference. I became so immersed in the music that everything else retreated to the periphery of my mind. In time this capacity to compartmentalise would be an effective way to survive a life that was destined to become increasingly challenging.

Through Mardi and Michael I learned more about the Greek and other philosophers and their different approaches to contemplating the universe and the world — Socrates, Plato, Aristotle and Hobbes. Our conversations often centred on Mardi's art or Jamaican politics. We talked about how women were, and are, invisible, and how they were seen, in the writings of Aristotle, for example, as belonging largely to the private realm of the household. The philosophical discussions helped me better to understand the relevance of what we meant in Jamaica when we spoke of creating a 'common good' within which all our people could participate and from which they could all derive benefits. In the early days those conversations with Mardi and Michael were often over my head, but I was always intrigued and listened keenly even when I did not feel confident enough to participate. I recalled Perry Henzell, my mentor and former boss, saying that I must always read widely to support what he felt was a wonderful mind. If Perry was the first person who believed that I was intelligent and that I should do everything to develop that gift, Michael was the second.

Michael and I would regularly discuss issues long into the night, after we had left Mardi and Regardless. He taught me never to leave anything unresolved before going to bed, so we strove for insight into what was happening with us personally and with the country politically. He encouraged me to give honest feedback, because resolution, he said, could result only through honesty. In return, I listened as he revealed the feelings of guilt, insecurity and inadequacy that plagued him all his life. We talked about how trusting he was of people, and how that trust was too often betrayed. He insisted on seeing the best in people until there was proof to the contrary. Michael expected people to keep their word and reacted angrily when they did not. He was quick to anger, and I often found his anger frightening. However, such episodes did not last long, and usually ended with him laughing at himself.

Michael was a perfectionist in all things, a legacy of his upbringing with Mardi, and this sometimes reached the point of obsessive compulsion about even the small things. For

example, he liked his comb on the left side of the basin and
would get very upset if anyone moved it even a few inches.
Dinner at his house was a formal affair — we always ate at the
table. I remember one night at Garth Road, early in the
relationship, when I cooked for him — I loved cooking for him
because he was such a big eater and a lover of gourmet food —
and I placed the water bottle right on the table. It was the first
time, and one of the few times, that he lost his temper with me.
A water bottle, he shouted, must never, ever be placed on the
table! Water must be served in a glass jug. If a grain of rice
accidentally dropped on the table that was another disaster. In
addition, he was easily embarrassed. Years later, when our
daughter Natasha was a baby, I couldn't take her to a restaurant
for fear that her noisiness or crying would make him
uncomfortable.

Yet I believe Michael too learned from me during our
relationship. I introduced him to Jamaican music, such as the
work of Bob Marley, Peter Tosh and Ken Boothe, and to Jamaican
foods, like stew peas and cooked-down chicken. He knew of
these foods but they had never been a part of his diet. He did
not like fish unless every bone had been taken out, because he
once had choked on a fishbone. He loved salt-fish fritters, ackee
and salt fish — salt fish done any style. Whenever he had salt-
fish fritters for breakfast, they would have to be served with a
pack of freshly fried bacon. The person frying the salt-fish fritters
would stand at the stove and serve him helping after helping
until he had had at least a dozen. He was mischievous at the
table, distracting us and taking food from our plates when we
weren't looking. Left to himself, he loved to eat and could eat

large amounts; he also put on weight easily. However, he took his health seriously, and keeping slim was important to him. He exercised regularly — in fact, he was one of the earliest joggers around the Mona Dam in the mornings — maintained a high-protein diet and drank alcohol only in moderation once he became prime minister.

Michael was also able to enjoy himself like no one else I ever knew. He would delight in walking in the mountains and admiring a rose, particularly one he had planted himself. He loved life. And I loved him.

Once my parents knew about our relationship, which was around the same time that I was officially introduced to Mardi, Michael had to meet my mother, who by then, strangely, had become a 'grass-roots' person. She was from a middle-class background; her grandfather had owned property in Jones Town since the nineteenth century and had bequeathed it to his son, Mama's father. This meant that my maternal great-grandfather and grandfather would have been permitted to vote even before universal adult suffrage in 1944; prior to that, only property owners were allowed to vote.

The youngest of three children, my mother was her father's darling and her mother's only child. Her mother had lived with, but was not married to, her father. As she struggled to manage my father, with his love of liquor and women, she rebelled by adopting more and more a working-class type of behaviour, even adopting the Jamaican patois that she had forbidden her children to use. She began to use violent expletives, and to be so forthright as to disregard the feelings of others. Nothing and no one fazed her. She considered herself perfect and thought

Beverley's parents, Eric and Esmine Anderson, at Beverley's wedding

Beverley, Edna and Michael, in the 1970s

Michael and Beverley, on their wedding day

Beverley and Michael at a PNP rally, their first public appearance as husband and wife

Beverley, in discussion with a women's group, 1970s

Entertaining Tanzanian President Julius Nyerere in the gardens at Jamaica House, 1970s

The Commonwealth Prime Minster's Conference in 1975, HM The Queen, HRH The Duke of Edinburgh, Sir Florizel and Lady Glasspole, and Michael and Beverley

Beverley with the late Coretta Scott King and Albert Manley
in Atlanta, Georgia

Greeting guests with Michael at Jamaica House in honour of former
Guyanese Prime Minister, Forbes Burnham

The Manley Family, Michael, Muriel "Auntie Mu" , Edna, Beverley and Rachel at a birthday celebration for Jamaica's first Governor General, Sir Clifford Campbell

Beverley and Fidel Castro (with his translator) in Cuba

Beverley escorting Trinidad and Tobago's former Prime Minister,
the late Eric Williams

Fidel Castro hosts Michael and Beverley in Cuba, 1970s

Michael, Beverley and PJ Patterson at the 10ᵗʰ anniversary Independence Day celebrations, 1972

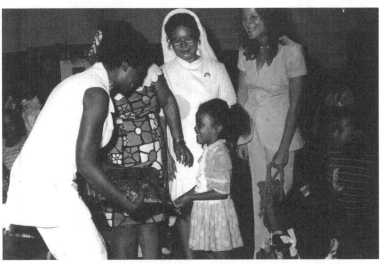

Beverley, Sister Benedict and Angela Melhado at Holy Family School

Michael and Beverley, shot for British Vogue

Carlene Kirlew, Beverley, Flo O'Connor (standing) and Maxine Henry-Wilson at a PNP Women's Movement press conference

Lunch with Rosalyn Carter at the White House

Daughter Natasha at the Sam Sharpe Square Rally, 1980

Official White House visit with President Jimmy Carter, 1976

Michael and Beverley at Bob Marley's funeral

Beverley on the air with The Breakfast Club

Mitzie Seaga and Beverley share an embrace

Myrtle Johnson, Beverley and Harry Belafonte

Michael and Beverly with Natasha and David

she was always right. Michael would not impress her. If it had been frightening for me to meet his mother, I never saw him having any sort of relationship with mine. Their meeting would be a challenge, I knew, because both were accustomed to being adored and getting what they wanted. I dreaded the moment and put it off until I was sure that I would marry him.

As fate would have it, I had no control over their first encounter, which was under the most unfavourable of circumstances. Michael and I had spent a long evening together and had returned to the house I shared with my sister Roma, and with Andrea Fletcher, my sister Shirley's sister-in-law. My bedroom suite was on one side of the house. Mama was spending some time with us while she supervised the refurbishing of her own house, which she had bought with money that she had saved over the years. I had invited Michael in and we were stretched out on the bed, chatting and enjoying each other's company with the door wide open. I was very aware that my mother was in the house; I heard her voice before I saw her, but was not concerned that she might embarrass me. Suddenly she walked right into the room and started to abuse us, calling us 'wutliss' (worthless) and saying that Micheal had no right to be in the house at that hour of the morning. As usual, I answered her back, giving her as much as she gave. But Michael asked me to let him handle it. He told her she was right but that everything was above board. He was not insulting her daughter. We were just getting to know each other. He apologised and said he would leave and that it would never happen again. After he left, I let her have it, but I was impressed at how well Michael had dealt with her. She in turn had appreciated his response and particularly his deference to her.

They did not meet again, however, until I had decided that Michael and I were in a committed relationship and that it was time she knew this. Only then did I take him to my parents' home on Rochester Avenue.

My mother was a great cook and knew how to entertain, but although she knew we were coming, she had made no special meal that day. It was to be business as usual. My father was warm and pleasant, but my mother made it clear to Michael that he was no big deal and that, in her house, he would do as everyone else did. He was to expect no favours. Michael just smiled and nodded, agreeing with everything she said. He was uncomfortable in her company at first but treated her with humour, and eventually they developed a relationship, which consisted mainly of her telling him how to run the country and the party. Much later, he would even telephone her when he became jealous of me or if I was late returning home. They were to become reluctant allies.

When I told my father about Michael, he wanted to be reassured that I knew what I was doing. He could not understand how anyone could be married three times, but he took his usual position on issues: he would allow me to do whatever I needed to do. I think he lived by the dictum that one should not cast stones. He was quietly supportive of the relationship, mainly, I believe, because I would be marrying a Manley. My father had voted PNP in every election and often talked about how he had been denied promotion within the railway because his support of the PNP was well known. Daddy had never asked the PNP for a favour and of that he was proud. He was the best of comrades.

In 1972, Michael and I decided to set a wedding date. We had had periodic discussions on the subject as early as 1971, but were both clear that we did not want to do anything to disrupt the political climate. Michael was sensitive too about this being his fourth marriage, so we decided to get engaged without telling anyone. He confided only in his best friend, Manley Macadam, a successful insurance salesman. While we were in Miami one weekend, Michael proposed and presented me with a diamond engagement ring. We decided that we would marry after the general elections.

Mardi invited me to spend the two weeks with her at Regardless before the wedding. At first the thought of staying there made me feel awkward, but we had come to know, like and accept each other. Michael approved of the idea; he felt that the invitation was a sure sign that his mother was in my corner. We decided that the wedding would take place in her back garden. I was delighted with the plan, as I had grown to love that garden, and Michael was pleased that I had chosen to get married there.

Regardless is a simple house with two bedrooms. Mardi occupied the room closest to the garden and I stayed in the guest room at the front of the house. Every day Mardi and I would go shopping, and in the evening Michael would visit, often for dinner but sometimes for after-dinner drinks. We often went to the theatre together, the three of us. I insisted that Mardi drive in the front seat. One night when we were returning from a show, she noticed graffiti on a bus stop: 'Michael is a fruit cake.' She smiled and said, 'I am always so happy to see something positive about my son.' Michael and I hid our grins and never let on he was being labelled a homosexual in what was a highly homophobic country.

Mardi talked to me a great deal about public versus private lives and issues of protocol. I watched her as she entertained, and marvelled at her graciousness and ability to hold a dinner party together. Ensuring that a party was a success, she told me, had much to do with whom you invited and how you seated them, and this required knowing as much about your guests as possible. The meal had to be just right, she told me, and it helped if everyone had something to drink.

Mardi warned me that Michel loved working out of his house although, she didn't feel that this was conducive to a healthy and happy marital relationship. She also said I should never get myself into a situation where I could not be available to Michael when he came home from what would no doubt be traumatic and often degrading political party meetings. To her mind, son and father were much the same. Michael kept close to people he knew and with whom he felt safe, men involved in politics, whether as fund-raisers, candidates or activists. Mardi tried to explain what public life would be like, painting a picture that boggled my mind. She had never really enjoyed it herself, she said, but had done everything she could to make Norman's life easier. I was alarmed at the thought that Michael and I would have little or no privacy. I would lie in my bed at night, alone in the guest room at Regardless, and wonder what my life would be like as a prime minister's wife. What I did know was that I wanted to use my position to help as many people as possible and to influence policies and programmes in my own way, particularly for women and children.

The wedding itself was on, then off and on again several times between February, when the general elections were won, and it was springtime. I had invited my two sisters, who were then living abroad, and another close friend. They all came, but then we decided to postpone the wedding because Michael was under a great deal of pressure from PNP colleagues and some businessmen. Who is this woman? they asked. Who is her father? The ceremony finally took place in June 1972.

Originally, Ivy Ralph had designed a cutwork linen train to be worn over a long sheath dress, but news of this got out, so I decided to ask Ruth Hussey, one of my designers, to create an embroidered cotton dress — peasant style with a triangular tie for my head. It was a simple dress worn with white satin court shoes. We told Auntie Mu; Douglas, who would bring his two sons, Norman and Roy; Gloria, who refused to send Sarah; and Thelma, who refused to send Joseph. I would have been happier to have Sarah and Joseph there, but Michael was not unduly perturbed. He felt that time would heal.

Michael and I went to Rachel's flat at Abbey Court the night before the wedding to tell her the news. We hadn't told her earlier because we felt sure she couldn't keep the secret, and so I had to lend her a dress at the last minute. It was one I had bought at Selfridges in London, when Rachel and I had visited earlier that year, an off-white cotton with a high neckline, tucks down the front of the bodice, and tied at the back. She looked very pretty in it.

Just before the wedding, Michael called the editor of the *Gleaner*, Theodore Sealy, and informed him of the wedding. Theodore insisted that the news should be kept secret for 24 hours, so that we would have time to leave the country for our honeymoon. Sealy asked him who the photographer was and Michael admitted there wasn't one. Sealy's reply was: 'If you don't have photographs, people will never believe that you are married — you know how Jamaicans are.' Michael and I discussed it and eventually I decided on Astley Chin, who had photographed me when I was modelling. When I called him I didn't explain the nature of the function. I just told him to come, and he did. And that is the only reason we have photographs of that day.

My wedding day finally arrived. Everything was in place. The officiating minister was the Reverend Ashley Smith. I was disappointed that none of my siblings could be present, but my parents were there. Mardi's home and garden looked particularly beautiful that morning. A small, mahogany antique table was placed on the patio with a white lace embroidered cloth. In the background, the Blue Mountains stood witness. It was as if nothing else existed outside of that relatively small space. When the time came, I made my way on my father's proud arm through the living room and into the garden to the strains of a love song by Roberta Flack. (Both Michael and I loved Roberta and later we would invite her as a guest of the government to give a concert in Jamaica.) It was the happiest moment of my life. As Michael and I faced each other to say our vows, we held hands in a grip that expressed love and commitment. We were sure in our hearts that we would be together 'till death do us part'.

Afterwards we posed for photographs in the garden and then enjoyed finger food and champagne. Later I changed into a pantsuit and we were taken to the Jamaica Defence Force Air Wing where we were met by Cabinet Minister Dudley Thompson, who accompanied us on the trip to Norman's Cay in The Bahamas and then took his leave. Our honeymoon was two weeks on that tiny island, where there were few people. Michael taught me how to fish, and we went fishing every day. I often cooked at night. Sonia Vaz designed my trousseau and I had at least two outfits for each day — a bikini, a matching cover-up and a head tie. Michael had insisted on the honeymoon. He said every marriage should begin with one. He was right. Michael and I skinny-dipped on the island, as there was no one to see us. I had never been in the sun so exposed before and I loved its warmth on my body, loved having the man I adored hold me.

Back in Jamaica, after the news of the marriage came out, some reporters found out where my mother lived and went to get her reaction. She refused an interview and chased them from her gate, saying only that Michael Manley was getting a good woman and the fact that he was prime minister meant nothing to her. When I heard about this, I was upset, but Michael had a good chuckle.

Too soon our blissful honeymoon was over. Dudley came back for us and we returned to Jamaica to a welcome at National Heroes' Park. There I met the party rank and file for the first time as Michael's wife. I was still basking in the glow of our wedding and time away. I was allowed to say a few appropriate words to the crowd, and was greeted warmly and enthusiastically. In his speech, Michael thanked the comrades for the warm reception on behalf of himself and his wife. This was met with loud applause. But he went on to warn those against his government, the privileged class, that he had received reports that they had already started to attack him, particularly over an increase in property tax. Although it was early in his administration, he said that he was ready for them.

It was clear to me then, if it had not been previously, that politics would take centre stage in our marriage. This just made sense to me. By then, I had been on the campaign trail with Michael for nearly three years. That politics would come first was okay with me, as long as I was an integral part of it. It was now up to me to chart my course. Some way, somehow, I had to maintain my identity while, at the same time, I gave myself up to Michael, as husband, party leader and prime minister.

Armed with Michael and Mardi's wisdom, but far from my own roots, I set off uncertainly on my marriage — a union whose possibilities, for both success and failure, seemed boundless.

Chapter 6

My first impression of Jamaica House was that it was a beautiful but cold edifice longing for love and care. There was nothing homelike about it. But Michael felt strongly that it was important for us to live in the official residence of the prime minister. The house, set on several acres of government land shared with the King's House, the governor general's residence, had been built in 1962 as a symbol of Jamaica's political independence. Alexander Bustamante, with his wife, Gladys, was the first prime minister to reside there.

The day we arrived to see the house for the first time, Michael and I entered through one of two entrances to the grounds — the official one on Hope Road, its wide gates opened by soldiers. I was completely unprepared for the soldiers, who were on ceremonial duty and clicked their heels in the presence of the prime minister. We proceeded past a long driveway to a fountain set on a circular mound, and we stopped in front of the house where two more soldiers stood guard. It was obvious at first glance that the house had not been lived in for some time, and that it would need a great deal of work. The previous prime minister, Hugh Shearer, whom I had met in this house the night Martin Luther King was assassinated, had hardly lived there, although he did use the house to hold official functions and meetings.

As I climbed the carpeted front steps to the house, I noticed that a veranda surrounded the entire building. Looking inside I could see a semicircular stairwell on either side of the main foyer. On the right side of the foyer stood an antique table beneath a gilt-edged mirror, and on the table lay a guest book. Despite the many flowering shrubs in the garden, I saw no floral arrangements in the house. As we entered, I saw to my left a room that I was told was called the Banquet Hall. Its focus was a large table surrounded by chairs and this room would prove to be one of the most useful in the house. From the right side of the foyer, a short passage opened into two anterooms for private secretaries and then a larger area that we decided could be used as Michael's study.

Past the front foyer was a small but delightful garden with hanging plants and a walkway that led to the back of the house. Beyond this I discovered another foyer from which a less lavish staircase rose to the second floor. To the left was a breakfast room that opened on to the kitchen and could also be used for small meetings. To the right was the formal living room, elegantly furnished with Queen Anne chairs, where the prime minister would entertain official visitors. But it was not the kind of room one could relax in. There were several sets of double doors to the veranda.

Michael and I loved to read, and so as we explored we kept searching for the library. We had thought that we would see at least some bookshelves in the living room. But there were none, so we kept looking. Was it possible that an official residence could have no library — no books? We didn't think so.

We ascended the stairs from the back foyer to the second floor, where we found yet another foyer. On one side was the guest room, on the other a long passage with three bedrooms and two bathrooms. This led farther down to a large bedroom with two balconies, one facing the back garden and the other the side garden. From the balcony, I could see the entire back garden of the house, acres and acres of it stretching to the boundary with King's House. Catching my eye at once was the outline of a map of Jamaica created out of a dirt mound in the garden, with various flora planted to distinguish one parish from the other.

By now we were getting excited about the possibilities for this huge house. We rushed out of the guest room and down the passageway to the other two bedrooms. The first had its own sitting room, and the second was at the end of the passage, tucked in a corner. This would become Joseph's room when he lived with us. Just outside this room was the stairwell that led to the kitchen downstairs, which would give Jo a private entrance and exit. Descending the stairs again, we entered a kitchen that was easily seven times the size of any other I'd seen. It was modern for its time, with stainless-steel sinks and a huge centre island. It never occurred to me to have it updated. It was not the kind of kitchen the average person cooked in, and I was intimidated by it at first. Fortunately there were also two chefs, a butler, and three or four helpers, to take care of food preparation not only for the family but for guests who would visit throughout the day to meet with the prime minister, as well as for larger groups of dignitaries. Outside housed the laundry area and quarters for the security staff.

Our first morning at Jamaica House I woke up and looked out the window, marvelling at the lushness of the grounds, which extended on all sides beyond where the eye could see.

Some parts were intricately designed with flower beds, others had been allowed to grow wild, resulting in exquisite surprises. Michael and I would often go jogging, and the air would be so fresh and clean that I couldn't believe I was in the middle of the city. I began to dream of all the things we could do with the grounds. A house on so many acres of land could meet some of the needs of the people. Later on, I would enjoy walking our daughter Natasha in her pram, listening to the sounds of the birds and the wind in the trees, and watching the dew settle on the greenery that surrounded the house. This, indeed, was paradise.

I remember Mardi standing on the balcony one day looking out over the land when it was parched by drought. I expressed regret at its appearance but explained we had to set an example during a water shortage.

'But there is so much beauty even in a drought,' she said, seeing things as ever through her artist's eye.

A group of workers employed by the Ministry of Agriculture undertook our landscaping. We took on different sections of the garden, including an area we called Baby Hounslow, after a state farm that had been established in Hounslow to encourage Jamaicans to feed themselves, where we planted vegetables and fruit that we distributed to family and friends. Hilary Matalon, wife of Eli Matalon, the former mayor of Kingston and St Andrew who later became a cabinet minister, helped us to reorganise the gardens. I remember her being on the grounds day after day. It was not unusual to have crops stolen from Baby Hounslow. Later Myrthe Swire-Coore, who was married to Finance Minister David Coore and who also lived in an official residence, Vale Royal, told me to be aware that some security staff would steal vegetables and fruit. In addition, with the help of Mrs Khouri of Federal Records, we started a small rose garden. I wanted the house always to be filled with offerings from the garden and so I organised Pearl Wright, an expert in ikebana, to train members of the staff in that Japanese art of flower arrangement.

Soon after we moved in, Michael and I set about redecorating the house and making it more family-friendly. I worked with professional interior designers, and despite how busy Michael was with his prime ministerial duties, he took the time to get involved, even helping to choose material for drapes.

We never did find any books, so one of the first things we did was to contact the Jamaica Library Service to take on this task. They did a great job. Based on conversations with Michael and me, they chose books, mostly on Jamaican history, politics and art, and catalogued them for us. We also decided to thoroughly reorganise the living quarters at the front of the house. The existing arrangement was four small rooms — two bedrooms, each with its own dressing area, and two sitting rooms. Michael and I loved a large bedroom, and because of his height he always slept in a king-size bed, so we had the walls taken down and created a large master bedroom and a sitting room with a small room off the side for a future nursery. The original master bedroom, a lovely room that overlooked the back garden, became our guest room.

Then there were the clothes cupboards. Living life in the spotlight requires one to pay attention to clothes, and that necessitates a large wardrobe. It was not unusual for me to change outfits two or three times a day, depending on the functions I was attending and the roles I was to play. We converted the existing closets into large ones with organisers — a place for everything and everything in its place.

Downstairs, we transformed the foyer outside the living room into a handy kitchenette, so that when entertaining there, we wouldn't have to walk all the way to the main kitchen.

Living in the prime minister's official residence was not without its challenges. It took some time to get used to having staff. Michael and I had had only one helper along with a part-time gardener and occasionally a day worker. Here I was at 31 years old, completely unprepared to manage a large house used for public events. Nor were the staff accustomed to having people in the house all the time, but they adjusted quickly. We all did. One of the first things Michael and I tackled was rectifying the working conditions of the household staff — all women at the time — who were paid by the government at minimum wage.

Another urgent task, as far as I was concerned, was creating my office. When we moved in, there was no such thing, but I intended to be an active First Lady. We were breaking new ground, so this was quite a struggle, but after discussions with senior civil servants, it was agreed that my office would be in a renovated section of the three-car garage. I wasn't particularly happy with this arrangement, but made the best of it, and counted myself lucky: I was the first prime minister's wife to be offered support services of any kind. I was assigned one member of the staff, Yvonne Rickards, as a personal assistant who did everything for me and with me, and who accompanied me, when necessary, overseas. I was also assigned a security officer. Another of my assistants was the remarkable Vera Hyatt, then married to Jamaican comedian Charles Hyatt.

Throughout this time, Mardi visited often, particularly when we had official functions — cocktail parties or dinners. We also had dinner regularly at her home. I kept my mother away from Jamaica House as much as I could, preferring to visit her on her own turf. I was too afraid that she might embarrass me. In any case, fortunately officialdom did not interest her. Michael and I spent some time socialising with his close circle of friends. But there was much to do and it appeared, never enough time.

We had one special place to which we sometimes escaped. Like his parents before him, Michael loved the mountains and needed privacy. Earlier his parents had built a small cottage, Nomdmi, on some land situated in the Blue Mountains, about 4,000 feet above sea level. When Edna suggested that Michael build a home on any piece of land there that he wished, he was overjoyed, and shortly after our marriage we used my savings to put up a tennis court. That was all we could afford at the time. We drew up further careful plans — we didn't want to have to chop down any trees and yet we wanted the best views — and over time built our own mountain home, which we called Nyumbani. Michael claimed that the word *Nyumbani* meant 'Welcome to my home' in Swahili, and we never questioned him on this. From Kingston we journeyed up narrow hillsides negotiating the twists and turns in the road, until finally we came to a forest of eucalyptus trees. Around the last turn and through a gateway, there was Nyumbani. Michael always said that when he was there he would look up at the sky through the trees and feel the stress leave his body.

Those first years of Michael's prime ministership were the Camelot years, years during which we had the support of a broad cross-section of the Jamaican people. Even then, however, we had begun to hear criticism from the upper class, which was upset that the administration had increased their property taxes. One of the first things the government did was to implement the Special Employment Programme, otherwise known as the 'Crash Programme'. Large numbers of women were given jobs for the first time, such as keeping the streets clean, and this in turn helped them to afford to care for their children. Michael's administration was also involved in Jamaica's first land reform programme, and in seeking equitable returns from our bauxite levy. The expectations of the masses were extremely high, in keeping with our slogan 'Better must come', the title of a popular song of the day.

We continued the process of building the party, and looking at all aspects of policy — financial, political and social — to assess what needed to be done, to decide what type of international policy would work in the best interests of the country. For example, internationally we opted for an enhancement of the policy of non-alignment, which allowed us to be encumbered by neither the United States nor the Soviet Union during the cold war. We were a sovereign nation and could take decisions based on our own national interests.

By my second year at Jamaica House I had begun to look for something more meaningful to do in my role as prime minister's wife. When Dudley 'D.R.B.' Grant, the father of early childhood education in Jamaica, called and asked to see me, I agreed immediately. Over the telephone he explained that he was deeply concerned that, despite all the lobbying efforts that had taken place, early childhood education was still being ignored. He wanted to discuss building the foundation for an efficient and effective education system. I was intrigued. When he came to see me in my office at Jamaica House he proceeded to inspire me in such a way that for the rest of my tenure as First Lady, and in fact the rest of my life, early childhood education would be one of my major priorities.

His proposal was this: Could I take the message of the importance of early childhood education across Jamaica? He explained that up to the early 1970s, government had played a supportive role in this, but the burden had been on the communities and the private sector. Accordingly, this area of education was unevenly managed, and often left to well-meaning but largely untrained women. He wanted the people to understand what Jamaica could accomplish if early childhood education were taken seriously. I needed no further prompting.

Michael encouraged me in the challenges I took on. He particularly liked this one because it helped children, because we were learning something new together, and because it represented something he could do in terms of policy. It also agreed with Mardi's advice that I should focus on something non-controversial, like children.

D.R.B. and I decided that I would start by observing teacher-training techniques and build my knowledge by reading the relevant research and data. Simultaneously, he arranged for me to visit most of the basic schools in Jamaica, to meet with the principals. Each time I visited a school, I took gifts with me, most of them donated by Jamaicans overseas — books and other learning materials, pencils, toys. I had the opportunity to see all types of schools, from urban and semi-urban to rural and deep rural. The buildings were often shabby, and the circumstances under which the students had to work inadequate. But I loved working with the children. I would look forward to their saying in unison, 'Good morning, Mrs Manley.' Teachers would often get the children to perform a song for me. The most popular one at the time was 'I'm a Little Teapot' — 'I'm a little teapot, short and stout. Here is my handle, here is my spout. When I get all steamed up, here me shout. Just tip me over and pour me out.' As they sang, the children would pretend to be a teapot, one arm akimbo as the handle, and the other held up as the spout.

The more I toured these schools, the more motivated I became to do all I could to ensure that every child in the age group three to six years was able to receive a good early education. I was impressed with women in the communities I visited, the often untrained, dedicated women who taught these children. Their contribution was a combination of sacrifice and service. After each of these tours, I would increase my efforts to work with these leaders and together make a difference.

D.R.B. Grant and I discussed the problems and possible strategies with Michael as prime minister and he immediately made arrangements for more government help in this area. As a result we were able to subsidise salaries and make training available for all teachers. In our search for ways to build awareness, we decided to get permission from him to build and operate a model school on the grounds of Jamaica House. This school, the Jamaica House Basic School, would set an example for the rest of society to follow and recognise the need to improve this area of education. I started to raise funds, and found the business community enthusiastic. Ancile Gloudon, the husband of veteran journalist and writer Barbara Gloudon, agreed to be the contractor, and Marvin Goodman came aboard as architect. The building was made of bagasse board, an inexpensive reconstituted product of sugar-cane waste. The school was based on a simple yet attractive design, with four classrooms, each with its own sanitary facilities, surrounding an open garden. The children were fed daily nutritious meals, cooked in a kitchen in the school building. The Ministry of Education supervised it, and we started with 200 children, and one teacher to every 20 students or so, assisted by teachers' aides. Teachers and children from other schools visited to see how the school was run. I was now able to visit and continuously observe a basic school in my own backyard. Marvin became chairman of the board and the school continued to operate until the PNP lost office in 1980. The construction of the school was in keeping with Michael's and my early resolve to make Jamaica House the 'people's house', and it is no exaggeration to say that starting that school changed my life.

The school opened on February 18, 1974, six days before I gave birth to my daughter, Natasha, and it remains open to this day.

Around the same time we were beginning to recognise the need to pay attention to children at an even earlier age than three, hence the propagation of the idea of day-care centres. In time, Nanny Day-Care Centre was built on the grounds alongside the basic school. Michael and I also encouraged women to create backyard day-care centres. The government would set up rules and procedures for their operation and parents would pay a nominal fee to have their children cared for in these centres.

In keeping with our commitment to make the house more accessible, we opened up the downstairs section to tours, particularly for schoolchildren. We also decided that the grounds should feature a garden theatre, a sports complex for young people, and a 'pocket park', a small area in which the children could play. I had learned of this concept from Señora Perez, the First Lady of Venezuela, when Michael and I visited there. Easton Lee, a family friend, actor and playwright, led a group that advised the government on setting up the theatre complex. Easton became a great friend of Edna Manley's and a collector of her art, and eventually was ordained a priest in the Anglican Church.

Early in my time as First Lady, I realised that the wives of cabinet ministers could be a critical group for lobbying and advocacy on a number of issues involving women and children. Among the group were women with a variety of skills, all of us the wives of policy-makers and involved in their constituencies. After meeting and thinking this through, we decided to form the Cabinet Wives' Association — in keeping with the Mao Tse-Tung concept that 'women hold up half the sky' — and our first project was a day-care centre in Kingston's industrial area. We believed that this would help us in our public education programme for the birth to six-year-old age group. Valerie McNeill, wife of the minister of health, and Yvonne Munn, wife of the minister of national security, assisted by other wives, decided to raise funds and build a day-care centre for the children of workers in New Port West. They would leave their children at the centre on their way to work and collect them on the way home. This concept was new to Jamaica, so we had to hold orientation sessions with businessmen in Newport West and, most important, with the communities surrounding the proposed site for the centre. We had to get the communities to buy into the concept and take responsibility for it, to understand its value and help to protect it.

The first session I conducted with businessmen was at Jamaica House. I chose my outfit carefully — a two-piece, off-white linen suit. I was extremely nervous. Who was I to be addressing these men? I was not even sure that they would come — but they did. I explained that increasingly women and mothers were entering the labour force. Once this happened, and there was nothing to stop it happening, society would be best served if our children had proper care, particularly during the formative years from birth to age six. I explained the three options: these centres could be in someone's backyard within the community, they could be public centres like the one at Jamaica House, or they could be in workplaces or industrial estates to serve several corporate entities. The last was what was being proposed for Newport West, Jamaica's industrial community.

The session went well. I backed up what I said with the necessary data. Most of the questions had to do with making sure that birth control methods were easily available to reduce the birth rate. These businessmen were also curious to know whether this would have an impact on female-employee productivity and their bottom line. I responded that there was proof in other countries that the impact of day care was not negative. These were new issues for Jamaica and so it was not surprising that we spent a long time discussing them. In the end, the group agreed to support the project financially, and I knew that we would realise the dream of building the day-care centre. The orientation meetings for the residents in the Newport West community focused on explaining to the group why they had a right to this type of benefit and the difference it could make, not only to their community but for the development of their children and Jamaica.

The centre functioned well for about one year. During that time we continued to meet with the community but, sadly, the centre was plagued by theft. After the refrigerator was stolen for the third time, we realised that we would have to give up the project, and reluctantly we did. We were all disappointed when it failed. I felt particularly sorry for Valerie and Yvonne, who had done so much to make it work. After that, I turned my concentration fully on the day-care centre and basic school at Jamaica House, and the influence that they could have closer to home.

In the meantime, Michael had asked the PNP Women's Auxiliary (later the PNP Women's Movement) to spearhead the backyard day-care centre programme in various communities. What was required was a clean space that met government's minimum requirements, and training for the caregivers.

And so from my vantage point at Jamaica House, my role was gaining a certain coherence. As President of the PNP

Women's Movement, I was entitled to represent the women in the party on all party committees. In addition, I was chairperson of the Political Education Commission and the Canvassers Training Programme and for a while was involved in the production of the party newspaper, *The Rising Sun*. Under my leadership the PNP Women's Movement became a radical organization and from time to time collaborated with Communist Women outside the Party to lobby for changes. I was concentrating on women and children's issues, not in isolation but as contributory to Jamaican development. Healthy, well brought-up, educated children would ensure a more successful nation. I made sure that in every policy of government this was taken into account. Sometimes my influence was through conversations with Michael, but it also extended to other ministries and departments. I had excellent support from those in the field immediately around me, as well as nationally, regionally and internationally. After the International Women's Year (1975) the United Nations declared the Decade of Women, through which all members were mandated to carry out programmes in the interests of women and, by extension, children. The government's institutional mechanism — the Women's Bureau — was in place, and we worked to revive the Women's Auxiliary in the PNP that would act as a vigorous lobby group.

I divided my time between the state and the party but always felt that I belonged in the party. I particularly enjoyed being with the people and working with them in their communities, giving them my love and appreciating the openness and affection they had for me. When we were building the Women's

Auxiliary, I would spend days on the road. Karlene Kirlew, whom we called 'Baby Councillor' because she was the youngest councillor elected to the Kingston and St Andrew Corporation at the time, was one of the hardest working people I knew. Nothing daunted her, and she was willing to do whatever it took to build the women's movement — even if it meant sleeping in her car when she was in a rural area and could not make it home to the city.

The Women's Auxiliary met with PNP women throughout Jamaica, listening to their concerns and encouraging them to form women's groups all over the island so that when we lobbied, we could do so from a strongly organised base. Simultaneously we raised the consciousness of men in the party. I made sure that Michael understood why the women's struggle was important for the country's development. As a genuine democrat he grasped quickly the concept of putting in place programmes and policies that did not discriminate against any group. That was the first step for him — it was a question of human rights and justice and he could understand that. From there, it was a natural progression to the realisation that so-called traditional areas of work for women and men had to be opened up to both genders and that, in any area where women were being discriminated against, the playing field had to made level.

My commitment to these issues was unwavering, no matter how they were trivialised and even when I was laughed at by some within and outside of the party. It got to the stage that when I led the women and would get up to speak in a party forum, there would be mutters from the group: 'That woman thing again.' I would keep a straight face and continue to speak authoritatively and with clarity, until, as Michael used to say, it all just made sense.

There was no doubt some in the party regarded me with a certain amount of suspicion. I collaborated with many members of parliament in their constituencies — and not only at election time. I was a hard and committed worker who was never interested in representative politics. People did not understand this.

Part of my job required that I travel overseas as the wife of the prime minister, either with Michael or on my own. On my earliest visit overseas, when Michael and I attended a Caribbean Heads of Government Conference in Trinidad, I met Erica Williams, daughter of Eric Williams, the prime minister of Trinidad and Tobago. I invited her to Jamaica and some time later she came as our guest at Jamaica House for a few days. She then invited me to Trinidad for Carnival. The media in Trinidad was intrigued by this 30-year-old First Lady with an afro. This was in 1972, before I had Natasha and when I still had my 'model' figure. Apart from press conferences and media interviews, I was photographed on every possible occasion. When I went for a dip at Maracas Beach, one of the newspapers ran a full-length photograph of me in a bikini. I decided to participate in a band, because Erica had explained to me that this was the way to really enjoy Carnival. After playing 'mas' in the streets with Erica and her friends, we appeared on the stage at the Queen's Park Savannah in Port of Spain. Eric Williams told me that when he observed me from the VIP box, he could tell I was not Trinidadian because I jumped far higher than I needed to — suggesting perhaps that I wanted to prove that we Jamaicans were truly Carnival players and could outdo the locals.

When Eric was younger he had played 'mas', but by the early 1970s he was no longer interested. It seemed that little interested him any more, and Erica was glad that he seemed to like me and that I had brought some excitement into their house. He was eccentric and lived in a separate part of the house, almost in exile. I never went there, and got the impression that few people did. One evening when we were on our way to an official function, I pointed out to him that people were waving and he should wave back. This role of 'reminder' was one I had grown accustomed to playing for Michael, who often became distracted. Eric Williams's response was that Trinidad people had stopped waving to him long ago and that they were obviously waving at me. When I was leaving Trinidad, Erica told me that she was glad that the trip had gone smoothly and that her father and I had got on so well. She could tell because he never unplugged his hearing aid when I was in his presence.

Early in my marriage to Michael, I travelled to Atlanta when the Jamaica Tourist Board was encouraging tourism from Georgia. Minister of Tourism P.J. Patterson (who would later become prime minister of Jamaica), led the delegation, when Michael had to pull out at the last minute. Anthony Abrahams, director of tourism and a Rhodes Scholar — someone I had met while my sister Shirley and her husband were at Oxford University — felt that I would add something special to the trip. Michael agreed, and so I undertook my first official trip on behalf of Jamaica. The Tourist Board's fashion guild organised my wardrobe and my main function would be to present Michael's message as guest speaker to a distinguished group at a dinner hosted by then governor of Georgia, Jimmy Carter.

By this time, Shirley and her husband, Richard, had returned to Jamaica to work in Michael's administration. Shirley worked for the Jamaica Tourist Board in their product development section, and Richard became a senator and junior minister in the Ministry of Finance. Roma came home from Miami and helped me in my office at Jamaica House for a while, as well as working in the Jamaican embassy in Cuba.

Shirley accompanied me to Atlanta, where my speech was well received and I presented Governor Carter with a painting by a Jamaican artist, a gift about which he reminded me when Michael and I visited him much later at the White House in Washington.

The itinerary for the trip was very structured. At breakfast, P.J. and I received many of the civil rights activists — Jesse Jackson, Andrew Young and Dick Gregory, among others. Later we visited Martin Luther King's gravesite and the church where he had ministered, as well as the Martin Luther King Foundation offices. Both Mrs King and Rev Abernathy accompanied us. I found Mrs King to be the most serene person I had ever met. I admired her for her composure and beauty and for what she was doing to honour her husband's name and work.

Having completed my official duties, I decided it was time to go to Underground Atlanta, the entertainment district, and have some fun. P.J. heard of my plans and vetoed them immediately. He told me that Michael had instructed him not to let me out of his sight. I couldn't believe what I was hearing.

Years later I would learn that Michael had given similar instructions to Anthony Abrahams, who also panicked when he heard that I wanted to go night clubbing. I felt loved and protected, but at the same time, controlled. I went anyway, and had a great time. When Michael found out, he was simply amused.

The other trip that stands out in my memory is our official visit to Cuba. I had heard so much about Fidel Castro, but the last thing I expected was a handsome man with kind eyes. There was something almost spiritual about him. I had never met anyone who had the kind of impact on me that he did. When I met him in the early 1970s he was physically fit and clad, as usual, in army fatigues, but I noticed that the olive-green fabric seemed to be specially made. It had a slight sheen to it and looked like 100 per cent cotton. I admired the fabric and as a result was given yards of it before I left Cuba. Although he understood English well, Fidel hardly ever spoke it. I soon learned, among other things, that, to friends of the Cuban revolution, he was 'Fidel' while enemies of the revolution tended to call him 'Castro'.

Fidel Castro gave an official reception for us. While we were waiting in the receiving line, he turned to me and said that as soon as we were finished, I should go to the bathroom and wash my hands. He explained that there had been many attempts on his life and that one such attempt involved poison being transferred to him through a handshake. As soon as the guests had all been received, we repaired to the bathrooms to wash our hands vigorously.

We stayed in one of the 'protocol houses' for VIP guests. Ours was Spanish style with white walls and beautiful hanging clay pots of a kind that I had never seen before. I brought some back to Jamaica with me and hung them in our garden, arranging them together, some high, some low. They always reminded me of our trip there. We also fell in love with Cuban ice cream, each rich and creamy mouthful caressing the tongue. After our first visit, Fidel would send us buckets of the delicacy. Later on, on his first official visit to Jamaica, Fidel became fond of Pickapeppa Sauce, cases of which we in turn regularly sent him.

Together Michael and I visited and were enchanted by Old Havana and drank margaritas in the bar whose claim to fame was that Ernest Hemingway had been a frequent visitor. We watched as Cuban women and men strolled along the promenade holding hands, eating ice cream. There was little or no crime in Cuba. I went to the nightclub Tropicana and enjoyed watching the exhilarating performances of the dancers, kicking their stockinged legs high. My delegation and I sang the only Spanish song we knew — *'Ay, ay, ay, ay, canta y no llores'* — and drank margaritas. I came away thinking, 'What a magnificent country!'

On one of our many evenings together, Fidel invited Michael and me to a small dinner. As First Lady, I had the honour of sitting next to him. He explained what we were eating and went into some detail about the cooking of each dish. He had an extraordinarily quick mind and seemed to know a great deal about almost everything. I also sensed some mischief in him. At one point when I had my fork to my mouth and was about to eat a piece of meat, he stopped me and said in English in a mysterious sounding whisper, 'Do you know what that is?' I realised that I hadn't thought about it, and asked him what it was. In Spanish he replied, *'Cojones, cojones'*, all the while laughing. I knew from my childhood that *cojones* meant 'balls' and in this case the balls of a bull. I put my fork down immediately and didn't touch *cojones* for the rest of the night. Fidel seemed pleased with himself!

I was not surprised that Michael and Fidel got on well from the moment they met. They both had great intellects, and they shared a sense of curiosity and a zest for living life fully and on the edge. They talked for hours, eating up each other's experiences, while at the same time understanding, respecting and accepting that history had bequeathed them two separate and almost irreconcilable ideological pathways, democratic socialism and communism. No discussion was necessary in this regard.

Although the Cubans knew Michael was not a communist, the courage and determination it took for him to be a prominent member of the non-aligned movement was not lost on them. He used every occasion to declare defiantly that the PNP philosophy of democratic socialism meant no alignment with either of the two world powers, the USSR or the United States of America. The Cubans also understood that Michael believed passionately in their right to choose their own ideology and to not be discriminated against because of this. They appreciated the way he stood up for them wherever he went in the world and knew the cost to Jamaica, especially the reaction from the US administration, which could translate into financial costs, for this stand. Fidel and the Cuban people in their isolation knew what it meant to have a friend in Michael Manley.

I was to make several trips to Cuba over the years, sometimes as the guest of the Cuban Federation of Women under the leadership of Vilma Espin, the wife of Fidel's brother Raul. I addressed mass rallies there. Gradually a friendship developed between the Cuban Federation of Women and the PNP Women's Movement, which spawned exchange programmes between us. On one of these visits, on a delegation that I led in the early 1970s but which had not included Michael, our group had gone to bed in the protocol house, known by then as Manley House, when a member of the household staff knocked on my bedroom door and told me that Fidel was coming. It was after 10:00, and he had not been expected. I was told later that arriving secretively in this way was one of his safety strategies. Excitedly I got up, changed into something appropriate, and rushed into the living room. I did not have to wait long. He arrived, looking relaxed. We talked about many things, about Cuba and about Jamaica. We talked about how the world was organised so that countries like ours were relegated to persistent poverty. The struggle, he said, must continue. As I listened to him speak, I saw Michael in him and thought how much these two leaders wanted the same results even though committed to very different methodologies. Of course, in the months immediately after the Cuban revolution, Fidel was committed to multi-party democracy. He now cautioned that Cuba's path was not an easy one and should only be taken as a last resort. We chatted through the night, and Fidel did not leave until dawn. When I got home and told Michael about this, he said that he was both proud and jealous of the connection I had developed with Fidel.

During another conversation with Fidel, as we talked about the workers' struggle, he told me that, as difficult as it was, it would triumph long before the struggle for women's rights. I was upset at the time by his words, but have since come to understand how correct he was about the intransigence of the movement for equality between women and men.

One of the many occasions that stand out in my mind with Fidel was when we returned from our official visit to Cuba. We landed in Montego Bay, the tourism capital of Jamaica. The PNP was contesting a by-election in Bethel Town, relatively close to Montego Bay. We felt it would be excellent support for the PNP if Michael had a public meeting in the west directly on his return from Cuba. Michael was to attend one of his political rallies, but this time it was fresh from a visit with Fidel and the Cuban experience. During his speech Michael mentioned that there were people in our society with a 'get-rich-quick-mentality' and that these individuals had a choice: they could stay, or they could leave Jamaica because there were 'five flights a day to Miami.' The media misinterpreted Michael's words. He insisted that what he had said referred to a tiny minority — what he called the 'clique' — who did not have the interest of the majority at heart, and would like the country to remain as a plantation economy. But he underestimated the impact of his own rhetoric as he stood there, six foot three inches tall, an imposing and mesmerising figure. The power of his words affected more people than he had intended them to, and, as a result, many followed their money overseas. For them, his statement was the last straw.

In those early years together, Michael and I also visited the former Spanish colony of Mexico. While we were paying an official visit, the International Women's Year Conference was being held in that city. The president of Mexico, Luis Echeverría, and Michael both addressed the conference and emphasised that policymakers must create the type of environment within which women could achieve their potential and therefore be full participants in development. During my tours with Señora Echeverría, we discussed women's issues and attended the closing session of the conference together as well as the Non-governmental Organisation Tribune taking place at the same time. During our tour of Mexico we travelled on a small, square bus of a type that I felt could be put to good use in Jamaica. I persuaded the president to donate one of these buses to the Sistren Theatre Collective in Jamaica, a group of special-employment workers, the ones who cleaned the streets, who used theatre to communicate their message, for example, the plight of household helpers and violence against women. This bus proved indispensable to Sistren in their early days, as they travelled between members' homes in Kingston and St Andrew. The group continues to be successful and has taken its theatrical productions around the world.

In keeping with the non-aligned foreign policy of the government, Michael and I also visited the USSR during the first term of the administration. We travelled via New York, where Myrtle Johnson-Abrahams, the then consul general and someone who had become a good friend, suggested to me that I would not survive the weather in the USSR without a mink coat. She had one and said I could borrow it if I promised to return it on my way back. She was right about the temperatures in the USSR: it was unbelievably cold and I was certainly not the only person wearing a mink coat! Even with the coat, I felt cold during open-air functions. While we were there we visited a number of historical places and spoke with senior members of the politburo. To Michael's and my delight, we were also able to attend a ballet performance. The government's Soviet Women's Group had planned a programme for me as First Lady which I enjoyed immensely. By the time I got back to Jamaica, however, *Gleaner* columnist Dawn Ritch had written an article titled 'In Borrowed Splendour', in which she accused the government of wanting constitutional reform rather than electoral reform, and in which she alluded to the fact that while I was in Jamaica I was for the masses, yet abroad I wore a mink coat.

Home from our travels, we never lacked for activity. At Jamaica House during the 1970s we hosted many functions in the backyard for dignitaries. The ones that stand out in my mind are Miriam Makeba, the Commonwealth prime ministers and their wives, Pierre and Margaret Trudeau, Erica Williams, Muhammad Ali (Michael was a big boxing fan, and his father and brother trained local boxers with Michael's support), George Foreman and Joe Frazier. In addition we hosted performances by Marvin Gaye and Roberta Flack. The most challenging of all the visits was that of Queen Elizabeth and the Duke of Edinburgh — I wanted badly for everything to be perfect, and in the end it was. Princess Anne too visited later. Guyanese Prime Minister Forbes Burnham and his wife, Viola, were among the few official overnight guests we had at Jamaica House.

By now I was getting a great deal of satisfaction from the initiatives in which I was involved. I received hundreds of letters each week, of which none went unanswered. Whenever I could help, I did, whether letter-writers were requesting school books or uniforms or items of clothing. I was enjoying most of the public part of my life, although it was not easy to eat so many of my meals with strangers. I was confident attending functions on my own and was equally pleased when Michael joined me, or I joined him. At the same time, however, I longed for the world I had once known, where I could just be myself and enjoy outings with my friends, without people pointing at me. Gradually, I was losing little pieces of myself. It would be years before I realised how much of me had disappeared.

I often felt very alone. Because of the life I was living and because of the schedule I kept, however, my private time was limited. I hardly saw my friends, and had to make a special effort to do so. Shirley travelled extensively and was often overseas. Public life, I soon found, was a lonely place to be.

Mardi never understood why Michael had to have a child with each of his wives, and why he seemed to lose interest in the child as each marriage disintegrated. Michael, for his part, was adamant that with our child, he would make up for his inadequacies in parenting his other children. He was willing to learn about parenting and make the necessary sacrifices, he vowed, particularly in terms of time.

While my first baby was growing inside my body, I talked to her, sang to her, listened to music with her and, most of all, experienced her movements and the amazing fact of a life unfolding within me. As her time within my body was nearing its end, her kicks became more and more powerful. I could see her fists doubled up inside me. Finally she turned her body out of the birthing position, and I knew that this was no ordinary child. She had already begun to display her defiance.

When I started having contractions, we called my doctor immediately and he told me to check myself into the hospital. The Caesarean section was scheduled for the following morning. Michael stayed with me in the private hospital, Medical Associates, which was run by Dr Burrowes, and despite being excited and nervous, I slept well that night, knowing that the following day I would hold my baby in my arms. Michael was more apprehensive than I was, given that his third wife, Barbara, had been diagnosed with cancer at the time she gave birth to Sarah. He never left my side, and asked the doctor endless questions about the operation. His was the last face I was aware of as I was wheeled down the corridor to the operating room. He was trying his best to look calm, but his anxiety showed. Shirley, who waited with Michael outside the operating room, told me later of the way he had paced the floor, driving everyone crazy.

The next thing I knew was when they told me that I had a baby girl. And there was Michael's face again; he was asking the doctor if we were okay. The doctor assured him that everything was fine, and the nurses passed the baby to Michael so that he could hold her.

Mardi had introduced me to Russian literature, including the epic *War and Peace*. I had fallen in love with the heroine, Natasha, and persuaded Michael that that was the name we should give our daughter. When she was born our child's head was crowned in black hair and her skin was the colour red of many newborns, though it would become bronze, similar to that of Michael's father's. Sadly, he would die before she was old enough to know him. This was definitely a 'Natasha'. Holding her for the first time in my arms, I marvelled at how innocent and vulnerable she seemed. I remember checking her body to be sure that it was perfect, and thinking to myself: 'Here she is, finally.'

Natasha's birth was one of the happiest moments in my life. There is no way to fully describe what it was like to hold my daughter in my arms for the first time. With her arrival, life suddenly seemed so full of promise. I vowed to give her all the love I didn't feel when I was growing up. I would manifest that love and be the perfect mother. Most of all, I was going to do everything possible to ensure that in spite of public life, hers would be as normal a childhood as possible.

It was during those first, seemingly idyllic months of Natasha's life that I first had confirmation of Michael's infidelity. I learned that he had been having an affair with a senior member of his staff who often travelled overseas with him.

I was shattered.

In confronting Michael, I insisted that the woman be dismissed from his staff immediately, and he complied. He asked me to forgive him, and I did. But I never forgot what I considered to be his first act of betrayal.

And I stayed. Of the two alternatives once offered by my mother — *you can be black and good for nothing like your father or you can be anything you want to be* — I had made my choice.

Chapter 7

Rachel was the first person to suggest that I should go to university. She always felt I had a good mind and thought that I should put on my jeans, join the undergraduates and make up for lost time. In 1975, after several discussions with Michael and sharing my thoughts with two women who were close to me, Sheila Graham and Jean Wilson, I decided to pursue what had secretly been my dream.

Sheila had recently graduated from the University of the West Indies as she had been searching for her independence within a privileged marriage. She encouraged me and insisted that, whatever I decided to do, I should study West Indian Literature as part of my university programme. It was excellent advice. She accompanied me to some of the lectures and guided me as a mature student returning to study.

Jean Wilson was employed at Jamaica House and had become my good friend. She wrote my speeches in those early years when I lacked the confidence to write them myself. She has this gift for getting inside the head of the person she is writing for. We discussed the speeches and agreed on what I wanted to say, and she got the content, style and language that was representative of me every time. She had also gone to university years earlier and her encouragement too included attending classes with me until I felt comfortable on the campus.

At that time, in the second half of the 1970s, there were few mature students on the campus. I was surrounded by youngsters. When I told Michael's security detail how excited I was about going back to school, the officer in charge questioned why I was doing this; people just took it for granted that I was already a university graduate, he said. I asked Michael if he was sure that the party and the country would not be embarrassed that the prime minister's wife was going back to school. He said that what was important was that he was proud of me, and that I needed to be confident and proud about it too. He also remarked that there were countless women and men in Jamaica who wanted to go back to school, and for whom I would be a role model. Particularly during the first term when I often felt inadequate, he was there for me.

My first morning on campus was particularly traumatic. By then I had a security officer who went with me that day, but I insisted that she remain unobtrusive. I had dressed in my blue jeans with matching shirt, trying to look like a student, but nevertheless, I was recognised and students stared in wonder. They talked about me, they giggled. Some of them asked in a loud whisper, 'Is it her?' I remember being so exasperated by the end of the day that I simply walked up to two students who were discussing me and said, 'It is me.' They laughed, looked embarrassed, apologised and supported me for the rest of the registration.

Many times during that first term I felt like quitting. The subject that I found most difficult was poetry criticism. I saw no point in it then, but I am glad I stuck with it. Apart from anything else, it helped me to look at words in a completely different way. After the initial struggle, words came alive for me. I began to understand that writers have reasons for choosing particular words and that the meter and style were also critical in understanding the poem.

Tutorials were particularly traumatic for me. The UWI is structured on the British system, in which students in a particular course come together for lectures, are given assignments and encouraged to use the library as much as possible. (I was fortunate because Michael and I by now had a fairly extensive library of our own, so my UWI library hours were shortened.) Once we had done the assignments we broke down into smaller groups of perhaps ten. A student would be asked to do the presentation and a discussion would follow. The group was so small that every student had to participate. All my inhibitions were on display and I felt awkward among all these young, often bright, people who had been studying all their lives. By the second term, however, I was participating much more and it was clear that all my practical experiences added value to the discussions.

My decision to study may have reflected a deep-seated yearning for a 'room of my own' — a private place where politics and the party could not intrude, yet a place that would afford me the opportunity to prepare myself to play my various roles in the public sphere. The UWI provided that space, and the students I met there were my support group. By the time I graduated and began the master's programme, I would invite some of them to join me for weekend study sessions at our home in the mountains. Michael welcomed these gatherings, and would sometimes join us, giving his perspective on the subject being discussed.

By this time I was beginning to understand the nature of the Jamaican economy, its structural imbalances and the ways in which it was integrally linked to the world economy. Slowly, too, I was coming to understand the interplay among gender, class and race. Most of all, I was gaining insight into social class and the role of what Michael termed the 'oligarchy'. As the political education programme continued within the party, coinciding with my study of political science on campus, as well as West Indian history and West Indian literature, my ideological consciousness began to sharpen. Within two years, I would move from the centre of the party to its left wing. This move would present many challenges for me, because increasingly I would disagree with Michael on strategy and tactics. Nevertheless, we found a way to discuss and work through these ideological disagreements, and he was open to my views, particularly those that came out of my own social class background. These differences of opinion were puzzling to some within the party who felt that he should just shut me up, and that my role should be relegated to 'suitable' activities, like cutting ribbons.

Michael and I always threw a party on New Year's Eve and 1975 was no exception. At these parties we got a chance to entertain the personal and political friends who continued to support us over the years. They were held wherever we lived — Jamaica House, Protocol House or, later on, Washington Close — and we usually had a wonderful time. One of the recurring happenings at these gatherings, however, was Michael's jealous rage. I had by then become accustomed to his outbursts, but they seemed to escalate after our marriage, particularly at parties, when they would spiral out of control. Very conscious as he was of the 17-years gap between us, Michael would say that he had only to watch the dynamic between me and another man to know there was a possibility that something could happen. Fortunately such rages were short-lived and disappeared as quickly as they had erupted. A smile would brighten his face and suddenly he would appear sheepish and apologetic. My reaction was always to remain centred and calm, perhaps because I had grown up dealing with my mother's rages. The storm would pass, and Michael was never physically abusive.

At one such New Year's Eve party, Michael drank more than usual. Late in the evening, when only a few guests remained, he suddenly lost his temper. I had been chatting with the few people who were there and there was no rational explanation for his jealousy. But then, rationality had nothing to do with it. He disappeared into the bedroom. A few minutes later I was sitting in the living room with Roma and her then boyfriend, when I saw him storming down the passage towards us, the front of his pyjamas, which were always missing their string, clutched to his stomach. He ordered our guests out of the house. As I quickly ushered everyone out, he aimed his attack at me. There was no reasoning with him, and I retreated to the guest room at the other end of the house, where a girlfriend was spending the night, locked myself in with her, and ignored his knocks at the door. The following morning he was like a lamb and apologised repeatedly. We talked things out, but that New Year's would not be the last time we would confront each other over his possessiveness.

Michael's jealousy was not the only thing I had to worry about in our marriage. We were now beginning to argue more and more about ideology, as I moved increasingly towards the left within democratic socialism and began to develop friendships with left-wing party members. I began to feel alienated from the upper classes and yet increasingly comfortable within the party. In some areas I was already taking on a leadership role, making speeches on various subjects, such as the issues of women and early childhood education, as well as party politics, and was representing Jamaica overseas. I had also become a close observer of the dynamics of the People's National Party as I attended meetings and had ongoing discussions with Michael. I had started to take an interest in Norman Manley and the founding fathers of the party, and was fascinated by the period 1938–44, when Norman Manley and his team left Kingston to go on the road and build the party, group by group. The first task was to sell the idea of a national party — to make the people understand why political parties were necessary. (Later, I would incorporate some of these early programmes into the PNP, including starting our annual conferences an evening earlier to accommodate an educational public session addressed by a special guest speaker, the first of whom was Gil Noble of ABC fame). Norman Manley had always intrigued me. I treasured that moment when I was ten years old and shook NW's hand after a public meeting in Rollington Town. It had a lasting impact on me.

Michael and I both knew from the outset that 1976 was going to be a difficult year. On January 2, we woke up to a morning like any other and went jogging at the Mona Dam. When we returned we sat down to read the newspapers. We always took two sets, so that we could read at the same time. I saw the story first. The *Gleaner* stated that 'unelected party activists' were now in charge of the government and that even the parliament was no longer supreme. Elected members of parliament were being bullied both openly and covertly, and were running scared. The *Gleaner* article claimed that the PNP was preparing for a Cuban-style communist takeover of Jamaican society.

We both realised that this story was intended to divide party members in an environment where there was already tension, often escalating into animosity, between its largely unelected left wing and the elected right and centre wings. It was becoming clear to us that the anti-communist hysteria that was being whipped up would form the foundation upon which the CIA, the JLP, and elements within the private sector and the middle and upper classes would carry out the opposition campaign. Michael's charisma was so powerful that even those who wanted to believe the propaganda, even those who wanted to hate him, could not help being swayed when they saw him speak, whether on television or in person. So there was a systematic attempt to tear him down personally, to chip away at his credibility. This was particularly so after columnists such as John Hearne, a long-time member of the Drumblair group and a Norman Manley supporter who had turned against Michael, and Wilmot 'Mutty' Perkins joined David DaCosta as columnists at the conservative *Gleaner*.

Subsequently, we learnt that the story had been written by the *Gleaner* editor, Hector Wynter, an ex-chairman of the JLP and one of that party's former candidates for a parliamentary seat. Hector had also served as a cabinet minister and diplomat under the previous JLP administration and was responsible for a great deal of mischief in some of his writing, such as Listening Post, a gossip column based on speculation and lies. Another such column was How Others See Us. These often scurrilous articles would be reprinted in the foreign press, increasing in number during the year leading up to the elections. Newspapers such as the *New York Times,* the *Wall Street Journal* and the *Washington Post* kicked into high gear. Previously any mention of Jamaica would focus on the bauxite levy that the government had imposed on foreign-owned companies. Now these articles centred on the impact of crime on tourists and in particular what they saw as the Cuba–Jamaica nexus. The pattern in the press, local and foreign, was to destroy Michael's image, to make him look like a man bent on bringing Cuban-style communism to Jamaica. The intention, we were sure, was to drive fear into the hearts of Jamaicans, particularly those in the middle and upper classes, many of whom were already leaving in droves. Any of Michael's utterances about Fidel and the Cuban people's right to claim their sovereignty, as well as speeches and sometimes press releases from the PNP Youth Organisation, were used to fan the flame of what the press, the JLP and the reactionary elements in society saw as the threat of communism. But the more these forces now aligned against us worked together to create and maintain the anti-communist hysteria in the country and the Jamaican diaspora, the more the PNP and its supporters were determined to 'stand firm'. The battle lines were decidedly drawn.

Despite my commitment and my conviction that what we were doing was right and just, I could not help being alarmed at what was taking place. I had grown up surrounded by conflict in my home, as a result of which I hated conflict of any kind. As a mother I worried particularly for Natasha. In times like these, as I watched her grow, I was especially reminded that everything we did had to be done keeping her generation in mind.

In January 1976 the International Monetary Fund and the World Bank held a conference in Kingston. Simultaneously, violence erupted in the western end of the city when armed terrorists burned sections of Jones Town and Trench Town. The violence that left hundreds homeless captured the attention of the foreign press who were in Jamaica to cover the conference. We began to see a not-so-invisible hand at work. The emerging pattern suggested some sort of systematic destabilisation, but it took Michael a long time to accept that. As the year unfolded, however, he would become convinced that there was indeed a hidden agenda. Crime was being used to strike fear into the hearts of the people in the hope that the government would seem out of control and thus lose its legitimacy.

But at the same time, positive changes were occurring. Gradually the social programmes of the PNP were taking effect and there was a new sense of pride and self-esteem among the masses of people who had been ignored for so long. Domestic helpers now had a minimum wage and the possibility of an eight-hour day. They were walking through the front door of the homes they worked in, instead of the back door. Political education classes were now widespread. Party members were being educated on their rights and, above all, the party school curriculum explained the nature of imperialism and of a world economy based on an uneven playing field, where workers were menial drudges in countries such as Jamaica, to use the Biblical image, 'hewers of wood and drawers of water'. The public consciousness was being raised. In addition, in keeping with our expanded foreign policy that said not all our eggs should be in the basket of the West — that is, the United States — party members were becoming more aware of the experiences of countries in the Soviet Bloc, Asia and Africa. Though still oppressed, the masses at least felt that their situation was being recognised and that something was being done about it. For the first time, they felt valued as human beings. The much-maligned Special Employment Programme was allowing thousands of people, in particular women, to feed their children and provide for their homes. The opposition complaint was that these people were lazy and were receiving money for little or no work, and there is no doubt that although the government did not intend this as a welfare programme, in many respects it turned out that way — although some facets of the original programme did evolve into more meaningful activity than keeping streets clean. The Sistren Theatre Group was one example of this.

Another change that created a shift in society was one initiated under the Status of Children Act. The majority of Jamaica's children are born out of wedlock and, under the original law, deemed to be bastards without rights. Under the new law all children were legal and had the same entitlements and privileges, whether or not born into a nuclear family, the product of a marital union. Mama's niece, my cousin Margaret whom we called Polly, was born out of wedlock, and over the years she would tell me how hard it had been for her. When she wanted to get into a particular school and she went with her mother, my aunt Myrtle, to be interviewed, the teacher bluntly informed her that they didn't take 'bastards'. She had never heard herself referred to in that way before, but knew it was a disparaging remark. She asked her mother, who explained. She remembered feeling less than human. That teacher could have been speaking to my own mother, whose father never married her mother. When I applied to obtain my grandmother's death certificate I found out for the first time that she and my grandfather had never married. I couldn't believe that my mother, my grandfather's pet, the favoured child, was as illegitimate as I knew her brother and sister to be. That teacher could have been talking to my older brother Tony, because my father never married his mother. She could have been talking to my sister Lilleth, who was conceived by her mother while my father was married to my mother. The teacher could have been talking to my first cousin Jeanette ... and I could go on and on. For these reasons and more, the Status of Children Act was one in which I took great interest and pride.

An area that made no sense to me whatsoever was unequal pay for women. Before the Equal Pay for Women Act, passed in 1973, women had grown used to the idea of such injustice; after all, most were already doing traditional chores in the home without any monetary compensation. Under this new law, women and men would receive equal pay for equal work, and employers were cautioned not to try to get around it by reorganising duty lists.

My mother's sister had started having children when she was a teenager. My cousin Jeanette had to discontinue her studies when she had her first child out of wedlock, at an early age. So many young women all over Jamaica saw their hopes for a good life dashed because they became pregnant. It was not a problem for the men, who of course could get on with their lives whether they were still in school or not. A group of us, including Lucille Mair and Peggy Antrobus, lobbied and got the government to set up Women's Centres so that school-age girls who became pregnant could have their babies and still finish their education. The babies' fathers were encouraged to attend the centres for counselling. Pamela McNeil headed and operated the centres for many years and under her leadership the programme was highly successful, with a repeat pregnancy rate of less than one per cent. Today there are seven such centres in seven parishes, from which 33,000 have graduated.

The minimum wage was another programme that meant a great deal to the 'working poor'. John Maxwell, a veteran journalist and supporter of the PNP, and our dear friend, shared with Michael his conviction that there was need for a minimum wage. Arising out of this was Michael's appointment of Dr Phyllis MacPherson-Russell, a noted educator, to head a team that would travel across Jamaica to enlist the participation of as many people as possible in deciding what the minimum wage should be. As a result of the National Minimum Wage Act, and for the first time in Jamaica's history, workers were to benefit from a wage based on an eight-hour workday, and the promise that this wage would be adjusted from time to time, depending on the country's economic conditions.

While we recognised the impact these programmes would have on the lives of the majority of marginalised people, we underestimated the impact of such social policies on the more fortunate and privileged in our society. In the case of the minimum wage, for example, many housewives would complain that, because of the eight-hour day, they now had to employ two helpers instead of one. Some vowed to 'turn us back' — in other words, to vote us out. The two sides — those who were the beneficiaries of the change and those who opposed it — were in direct conflict.

No matter how things looked on the ground, Michael believed that we should not allow propaganda to force us into early elections. We expected that the work for the campaign would have to be heightened early in 1976 if we were to win the following year, but not that elections would be called before 1977. As the year progressed, however, Seaga and the opposition JLP campaigned increasingly for early elections. A major plank of their campaign was to paint the PNP and Michael Manley as corrupt, especially in the way they handled and criticised the media. Another widely aired grouse was the PNP's 'mismanagement' of the economy. Seaga placed himself firmly before the public as a 'financial wizard', a claim made credible by his many pronouncements about economic doom, often based on confidential documents purloined from the Bank of Jamaica or the Ministry of Finance. These leaked documents made it appear that he, and only he, knew what was happening. Michael was particularly angry about the leaks; he could not understand the character of the public servants who were prepared to be dishonourable and dishonest, nor the nature of people who would use such information for their own biased purposes.

If there was a human being Michael Manley detested, it was Edward Seaga. He felt Seaga had no scruples whatsoever and was the worst thing ever to happen to Jamaican politics. Michael shared this sentiment with NW who, in the late 1960s, when Seaga entered politics, was quoted publicly in a PNP publication as saying that something 'evil' had entered the political process.

By the middle of the year, Seaga and the JLP often had the PNP on the defensive. Violence — murders, rape and arson — provided the climate in which the foreign and local press attacked us. They singled Michael out as the head of a political party gone crazy, one that accepted Cuban communism as a way of life. Implied, if not explicit in all of this, was the domino effect. The United States and their local allies believed that if Cuban communism could spread its wings into Jamaica, this would, in turn, permeate other areas of the English-speaking Caribbean. To assuage some of these fears, Michael always ensured that the minister of industry was a private sector man and therefore someone they could trust. The State Trading Corporation (STC) took over the function, previously assigned to the private sector, of importing basic necessities: food, drugs, and materials for the construction industry. The corporation originated out of another entity, Jamaica Nutrition Holdings, an agency involved in importing basic food items for the poor. The STC extended this to include other items for the poor, cutting out the middleman so that they could be offered at a reduced rate. Private-sector merchants who had previously been involved in these imports were upset. The person placed in charge, OK Melhado, was also a private-sector man. He and his wife Angela were our close friends and they belonged to the wealthy class. This hardly helped, as day after day the private sector and the *Gleaner* criticised the STC because it was cutting out private-sector middlemen, another initiative in the interest of the masses that would threaten and therefore inflame the commercial sector, setting the society against itself.

In response, the private sector formed an umbrella organisation, the Private Sector Organisation of Jamaica (PSOJ). Its founding president was a patriot, Carlton Alexander, who genuinely wanted to protect the interests of the business-based private sector through ongoing dialogue with government. However, other elements in the organisation, such as the president of the Chamber of Commerce, Winston Mahfood, were JLP supporters bent on using the PSOJ to defeat the government. Later, in the 1980s, the two founding directors, Anthony Abrahams and Anthony Johnson, would become cabinet ministers in the JLP administration.

At the organisation's launch, with the governor general present, a group of PNP women under the leadership of Valerie McNeill disrupted the proceedings, conversing among themselves, responding loudly to what speakers were saying, and generally making it clear that they felt the PSOJ was designed to oust the government. The PSOJ executive director was forced to cut the meeting short.

Even as internal conflict in the party continued, the party secretariat under D.K. Duncan's leadership enhanced its political education programme. Party members and officials were not aware that the economic situation was reaching crisis proportions. The job of those of us in the secretariat was to keep the party highly mobilised and organised. The cabinet, and in particular the minister of finance, would take care of the rest. The prime minister, the minister of finance, the governor of the Bank of Jamaica and the head of the Planning Institute of Jamaica knew what was happening in the economy, but the extent of the problem was never shared in detail with the party.

As crime and fear increased, Michael began to meet every day with the country's security forces. Never before in the history of Jamaica had class conflicts, and therefore racial friction seemed so raw. Women's consciousness too was on the rise. The women's movement, including the PNP Women's Movement, grew more militant, in keeping with what was happening in the global women's movement during the decade 1975 –85.

The Manley administration was fighting for its life. Michael struggled to have the left and right wings, now two ideologically opposed forces, work together using his tremendous consensual skills, honed during his years in the trade union movement. To the left wing in the party and the communists outside it, under the leadership of Trevor Munroe, it was obvious that there was destabilisation in Jamaica in which the CIA was playing a leading role. This belief was based largely on what had happened in other countries, such as Chile under Salvador Allende, a scenario studied closely in Jamaica because there appeared to be many points of comparison. In the case of Chile, Allende was saying that all he wanted from Chilean copper was that every child in Chile could drink one glass of milk a day. In Jamaica, we wanted to earn more for our natural resource, bauxite, for the same reason.

Although increasingly the conservative elements inside and outside of the PNP were deeply concerned about the rise of the left wing, in fact the left was dominant for a relatively short period of time, from 1976 to the end of January 1977. But even within the party a familiar and ongoing question from the right wing was, 'Are we going communist?'

As tensions in the party and in the country heightened, Michael and I continued our nightly conversations on matters of party and national importance. He was worried about party unity. He was concerned about the economy, and about the mounting crime. He wondered who was instigating the violence. He did not want to believe that it was the United States through the CIA as he couldn't see at the time why the PNP's programme and its policies would attract that kind of attention from the US administration. Surely the Americans could see that changing the balance of power in Jamaica was critical to our survival, and that it made sense to ensure the majority of Jamaicans had the basic necessities of life. We talked about the history of US involvement in the Caribbean and Latin America. I was in the middle of my undergraduate programme at UWI, and some of my lecturers were communists, including Trevor Munroe, who was also the head of the Workers' Party of Jamaica (WPJ). Trevor would strut into the classroom and hold his audience rapt with his lecture style and, at least in the case of the women, his tight jeans. He analysed our current Jamaican experience in terms of the class struggle central to Marxist–Leninist philosophy.

The communists did not think much of 'mouth-water' democratic socialists, as they called us. For us, the distinctions between them and us were very clear. They believed in the Leninist concept of communism where power was centralised and concentrated in the hands of a few. We were democratic and believed in increasing democracy from the bottom up, including at the level of our communities and in our schools.

They believed in class warfare while we believed in the critical importance of the class alliance. They had no desire to cooperate in any way with the imperialist United States, whereas we believed that we had to find ways to convince the United States that they should do something about inequality in the world, if only because it was in their interest to do so. The PNP Youth Organisation in its fervour often came out with statements extolling the glories of Marxism–Leninism. The PNP was quick to deny these statements and, in at least one case, the party disciplined the Y.O. leader, causing its entire executive to resign, claiming collective responsibility. They remained members of the PNP, however, as they still saw it as the only vehicle that could deliver justice to the majority.

Despite the escalating violence, the party did not at first entertain the idea of declaring a state of emergency. Jamaica did not have the type of intelligence apparatus needed to determine who should be detained. Michael was also concerned about what a state of emergency would signal to the outside world, especially its impact on the tourism industry, which was already reeling from negative statements in the foreign press. By the middle of 1976, however, the situation was out of control. The incident that tipped the scales was the murder of the Peruvian ambassador on June 14, 1976. The security forces assured Michael that they were prepared, and one week after the murder, on June 19, 1976, the government declared a state of emergency. There was at first a decrease in homicides, and there were many arrests, including that of a prominent member of the Jamaica Labour Party, Pearnel Charles. The government did everything possible to allay the fears of the opposition and of the United States. The tourism industry, as we had feared, was affected. The newspapers overseas carried articles warning Americans not to visit Jamaica. But we had the support of the majority of the Jamaican people, as revealed by national polls: upwards of 80 per cent supported the state of emergency up to November 1976.

By now, the *Gleaner* had appointed a new managing director, Oliver Clarke, a powerful landowner and businessman. Within a month of taking office, Clarke would be elected to the executive of the Inter-American Press Association (IAPA), an organisation publicly associated with the CIA. We knew that the executive board had four members from *El Mercurio,* the Chilean equivalent of the *Gleaner* that had played a critical role in the ousting of the Chilean president, Salvador Allende. Ten days after the declaration of the state of emergency, Michael brought up in parliament the subject of a plot to overthrow the government under the name 'Operation Werewolf'. Adding fuel to the fire, Michael was under pressure from the opposition forces to call the general elections. The Secretariat was preparing for elections in two years time.

After discussion within the party, Michael decided that he would call early elections so that the Jamaican people should have an opportunity to decide on economic policy. This time around, instead of accompanying Michael on his campaign tour, for the first time, I would have my own tour. It was not unusual for us to say goodbye to each other at the steps of Jamaica House, hug each other and hope to see each other alive at the end of the day — Michael then going in one direction and I in another. It was a dangerous campaign. Strong leaders, who were aware that this was more than a general election, led both political parties. It was like a stage upon which the cold war was being played out. As the intensity of the PNP and the JLP increased on the campaign trail, so did the country's violence. Michael and I never left Jamaica House without seeing that everything was in place — especially to ensure Natasha's well-being — in case either of us was killed. But politically, there was now no turning back.

The elections were slated for December 15, 1976. Four months earlier at the party's annual conference, Michael had declared to thousands of comrades at the National Stadium, 'We are not for sale.' In other words, no one would ever again tell Jamaica what to do. Those of us who worked in the PNP secretariat took Michael's annual conference presentation seriously and began to mobilise party members and supporters around it. The conference had at first been scheduled for the National Arena. D.K. Duncan, the general secretary, made arrangements for it to be moved, if necessary. As soon as the National Arena was overflowing with comrades, he announced dramatically that because the arena could not hold the large number present, Michael, party leader, would lead us to the other venue. He gave the signal, and the people rose, as one, to their feet and, in a disciplined and orderly manner, followed their charismatic, anti-imperialist leader across the street to the larger 20,000-seat National Stadium.

History was to be created that day. Here was a defiant organisation that had gone through fire, now standing up to the United States and its local allies in the JLP, and to the conservative elements who wanted to turn us back. Michael was nervous. He was about to stand at the front of a bandstand with thousands of people before and behind him. Like any great communicator, Michael was always concerned that the sound system was good. He had come a long way since his earliest union days, when he would speak to workers at the factory gates equipped only with a bullhorn in his hand. On the campaign trail, depending on the constituency in which he was, the sound was often bad and his vocal cords would be ruined for the next event. He knew that he could talk to the masses and workers like no one else could. He knew what he could do with a message. D.K. assured him that the sound system was the best available. Now the militant, enthusiastic and adoring crowds were waiting. The stakes were high.

Michael wanted to be articulate for this crowd, wanted them to be clear about the policies and programmes of their government and party. They had to understand why the times were so hard and, most of all, why they must stay with the struggle until they could see the light at the end of the tunnel. He told me that he did not know how to address a crowd that surrounded him. Knowing his flair for the dramatic and his love of theatre, I whispered back, 'The whole time you are speaking, just think of the concept of "theatre in the round" and turn as often as you can to include all members of the audience.' He got it immediately. The other thing he was concerned about was how to tell the comrades that many more hardships were on the way, how to convince them their suffering was not in vain. It suddenly occurred to me that, based on my own experience, I knew that suffering as an end in itself is merely suffering, but that suffering merely as the means to an end, for a cause that means justice and equality for all, is quite different, for it is suffering with a purpose. Michael took this and presented it in his script exactly as I had said it to him. All the time we were talking, comrades were coming up to greet us and the speakers were warming up the crowd for the leader's presentation.

Convinced, finally, that the sound system would allow a mere whisper to flutter effectively across the sea of people, Michael climbed the stairs of the grandstand to tumultuous applause, the mountains providing a dramatic backdrop. The applause continued until he raised his right hand to still the audience. Out came the Rod of Correction, which he said had been given to him by Haile Selassie. For the people, the rod — Joshua's rod — evoked memories of our African ancestors and this added a mystical quality and a sense of black pride to the proceedings. I had been put in charge of the safety of the rod and took my task seriously. Each time Michael went on the road, the rod would be taken out, and after the meeting, it would be returned to its place of safety in Jamaica House. Now Michael held up the rod with arms outstretched, swinging it first to the right, then slowly around in front of him in a semicircle, then to the left and then finally back to the middle of the arc — shaking it periodically for effect. The crowd was ready to eat out of his hand. Eventually, he held the rod still and the crowd calmed down enough for him to say 'Comrade Chairman', and the applause began again.

We were particularly pleased at the turnout of the middle class, as part of the propaganda against the PNP was that we had lost the middle class, the foundation on which the party had been built. In addition, Michael was concerned about a perception that he had betrayed his own class. I can hear him now, as he said in his speech, 'Look around you — who do you see? Look around you, look around you', again to riotous applause as the crowd acknowledged the middle-class presence. Jean Wilson, a communications expert who had worked with us from as early as 1974, and I decided that very night that we would create a long-playing record of the speech interspersed with party songs. The suggestion had come from John Maxwell, a journalist who supported the party and was Michael's friend. We were so blown away by the occasion — the location, the militancy and courage of the people, and Michael's inspiring presentation — that we headed off to Dynamic Studios just 24 hours later. That was the kind of energy created that night. Working tirelessly, within two days we had produced an edited version of the speech. Within the week, the record jacket had been designed, featuring an inset of Michael with the crowds around him. On the back cover we printed the moving finale of the speech, what Jean referred to as 'the first poem of the revolution', in which Michael asked us, among other things, to consider the children of Jamaica.

Everywhere we went during the election campaign, supporters would play the record and Michael's voice would boom out the militant, anti-imperialist message as comrades sang lines such as 'No turning back, no turning back'. One of the JLP slogans was 'Turn them back'. Reception to the record was enthusiastic. At the same time, a young man by the name of Neville Martin had written a song highlighting the social achievements of the PNP since taking office in 1972. The refrain of the song was 'Juk Dem' — meaning 'sock it to them'. One line from the song was 'Juk dem wid free education'. After D.K. heard it, he arranged to have several copies made for each constituency. I remember I was in the parish of Westmoreland, campaigning for a female member of parliament, Carmen McGregor, when I first heard the song. Here was a song that for comrades captured everything they felt about their party and why they so strongly supported it.

As election day approached, it seemed that we had everything we needed for a decisive victory at the polls. Seaga had earlier publicly claimed that the PNP was involved in discussions with the IMF and that the party had already agreed, if we maintained power, to a massive 40 per cent devaluation and a wage freeze to take place immediately after the elections. But the government was quick to deny this. The consensus among comrades was that this was Seaga's wild imagining at work — Seaga, as the Prophet of Doom.

Though the campaign took place under a state of emergency, there was no evidence of any constraints or limitations, for example on the freedom of the press, because of this. The fact that the Stone Polls consistently showed support for the state of emergency, did not, however, prevent the opposition JLP from thinking that the state of emergency would be used to lock up their members. The PNP gave assurances that it would not be misused in a partisan political way. However, in an atmosphere of such heightened tribal tension, their anxiety was understandable. Although the opposition campaign focused on communism and the economy, the state of emergency did not seem to be an issue.

The PNP manifesto promised a programme of constitutional reform with public discussion and participation. Michael was at his most militant and courageous during that campaign, and my love and admiration for him increased exponentially as he made his way from parish to parish, from community to community, walking, carrying out house-to-house campaigns, pressing flesh, hugging people, day after day after day. Michael's speeches reflected the reality of the violence the country was experiencing even during the state of emergency, as he called on comrades to put everything into the struggle against the reactionary forces. The party must be united, with all its members working as they had never worked before. Our platform speeches, in keeping with the 'Not for sale' theme, emphasised the role that imperialism and the 'clique' — the oligarchy — played in the day-to-day life of every Jamaican. Michael spoke of the New International Economic Order (NIEO) and the need for equity between trading partners. We must begin to get prices for our sugar that could pay for the tractors we import, he said. Most of all, he maintained, Jamaicans must choose the economic path they wanted so that the society might be based on justice and equality for all. I can hear him now as he refined his speeches. He derived his energy, insight and courage from his audiences, who hung on his every word.

The PNP also focused on its first-term programmes that laid the foundation for all the people of Jamaica to have a better stake in their country, no matter who they were. As Michael hammered home these themes, he explained in language the masses could understand that the PNP's principled foreign policy provided the framework for its domestic policy, hence the need to have a non-aligned foreign policy of the kind that opened up Jamaica to what was happening in the entire world, including the communist bloc. A vote for democratic socialism was a vote for more even distribution of power between the haves and the have-nots.

Our efforts and those of the rest of the party began to pay off. During the last six weeks of the campaign it became clear to us not only that we would win but that the result would be a landslide. It wasn't just the size, but the nature of crowds, committed and unflinching. They seemed willing to fight to the death — if that was what it took.

December 15, 1976. Election Day. Michael and I drove through the countryside, reflecting on and discussing the campaign activities and just being together. He was relatively calm. He knew he had done everything he could to secure a victory. It was now up to the masses and, as a democrat, he would respect the people's decision. We went to bed immediately after the polls closed. I lay beside him for a while and we talked, reviewing the struggle from 1969, when he became party leader, to the present. We talked about how far we had come, the many challenges we had faced, and the ones we would face now. It was an intimate moment, an open and honest conversation between husband and wife — or so I thought at the time.   ᵛ

We were both exhausted, physically and emotionally, from the campaign. The polls closed at 5:00 p.m.; votes were being counted; there was nothing more we could do until the results were in. Eventually I left him alone for a couple of hours to rest and reflect. Two hours later, I woke him with the news. The PNP had won 47 of the 60 seats in parliament, polling 56.8 per cent of the popular vote to 43.2 per cent for the opposition JLP. A record 85.2 per cent of the voters on the list had voted. The PNP had increased its vote from 36:17 to 47:13.

We had done the impossible. The victory was beyond our wildest expectations, and it was what we needed to take the struggle forward.

We didn't have to wait long for the opposition's reaction. Seaga, in accepting defeat, said, among other things, that never before in the history of Jamaica had the people spoken so loudly and so clearly. He seemed to speak from the heart, but within a couple of months his position would change. The JLP would challenge results in several of the seats and start to put doubts in people's minds about the degree to which an election could be free and fair when held under a state of emergency.

Michael, for his part, asked all PNP supporters to accept the victory quietly, avoiding any loud celebrations. To a large extent, the people complied. I was not sure of his reasons for this, but I went along with him. The family — his children, his mother and brother — came to our home and shared the joy of victory. But everyone knew that we were in for a tough time. We were going to have to redouble our efforts to remain in office for that second term. Michael and I talked at length that night before falling asleep, and reconfirmed our commitment to the political struggle and to our marriage.

A few weeks later, a US official, in referring to the victory, told me that he hoped that I realised that by winning, we had moved to another page in the US State Department book. These ominous words chilled me, and would return to haunt me many times in the months to come.

Chapter 8

A few weeks after the 1976 election, Michael walked into our home at Hopefield Avenue, his long strides dominating the pathway from the garage and into the kitchen where I awaited him most evenings. He always returned sometime between 6:00 and 7:00. He signalled to me to follow him into the bedroom. Taking two quick steps to every one of his, I was almost running to catch up. As usual, I was so admiring of him. But what on earth could be on his mind? I asked him and his response was that I must wait until we got to the room. Suddenly I had a sense of impending doom.

In the bedroom, we sat next to each other on his side of the king-size bed. I was aware of the vastness of this space of ours in which we had cuddled and made love and talked and ironed out our problems. Dramatically, he held both my hands and told me to brace myself. I wondered then if he had met someone and wanted to leave the marriage — the atmosphere held that kind of tension.

He said that he was calling on me for a loyalty that, up to then, he had not asked of me. I had begun to understand his concept of loyalty and to know that the term 'political loyalty' had a particular meaning: blind faith. But I had long since passed that stage. My trust began to erode the first time I realised that Michael had been unfaithful to me. I stayed with him because I loved him, because I had a newborn baby and, most important, because D.K. Duncan had convinced me, someone I hardly knew at the time, that the struggle was much larger than my personal life and that it was critical that I remain at Michael's side. Michael had sent him to talk to me, D.K. said, because he knew how much I wanted to be part of the left wing of the party, many of whose members came from a similar class background to mine.

'Take a deep breath,' Michael said, 'and listen to me.' That was when he told me of the impending IMF agreement. He knew that this was an organisation of which I was highly skeptical.

My first brief reaction was one of relief. He was not leaving me for one of his women. My next thought was that perhaps Seaga had told the truth about the PNP's secret negotiations with the IMF. But no, the government had flatly denied that it was involved in such discussions. At that moment I just wanted to know the truth, I didn't want it prettied up. I remembered my mother saying how she hated hypocrites, people who skirted around issues. Tell the truth, she would say, cost what it may. My husband seemed to want to tell me the truth, to need to do so — but clearly he didn't know how. I had never seen him so uneasy.

Finally, Michael admitted that secret negotiations had been held with the IMF before the elections so that, if the party won, the government could take up the IMF option. So there it was. Seaga had told the truth. Michael had lied. As his wife, I had accepted his infidelities because of the bigger picture, because

I had respected what he was trying to do for Jamaica. But now I could see that the leader had feet of clay. At the time, I was very judgemental of him. He had taught me everything I knew about ideology and politics. Looking back I realize, though I don't agree with the decision he made, and that it cost the movement dearly, there might be some naïveté in the view that anything in leadership is cut and dry or that simple. He was, in fact, caught in a conundrum that even the most well-meaning socialists get caught in when the powers that be, which are economically conservative and hold the purse strings, lean on you. I realize he was not meaning to crush the dream, but didn't know how else to rescue it. He was almost doomed to failure, unless he took Cuba's path of resistance, and by then there was no benefactor like Russia to help him through if he did. He had grown tired of being persecuted. He just couldn't do it anymore. I realize now that that one moment was not the sum of his worth as man and as a public servant.

That night Michael went on to explain to me the nature of the crisis within the party: the left wing now knew that they too had been told less than the truth about the IMF negotiations. He was talking to me as his wife and as a leader of the women's movement. As his wife I would have to provide the personal support he needed at this time of crisis, and as a leader in the women's movement I would have to put the party first, keeping his credibility and that of democratic socialism intact, while explaining to the women of Jamaica what the agreement would mean to them. I didn't see how this would be possible. I knew enough about the IMF to be sure that the first group to feel the negative impact of any agreement would be the women.

As I listened that night, I remembered well Mardi's advice to stay away from the party politics so I would be there for Michael when he needed me most. But I had not stayed away. She was right: when he needed me, I was not there for him, not in the way he wanted, not in the way his mother would have been there for his father.

I was enough of a politician by then to sense danger. In the months and years that followed the revelation, the more I learned about the likely impact of an IMF agreement on the majority of Jamaicans, the more distraught I became. The masses had voted for the social programmes implemented during the PNP's first term. If democratic socialism meant these programmes, they were what the masses wanted. An IMF agreement would derail these programmes. Under IMF programmes, the people were not the priority.

I was deeply troubled, not only for me and for Michael, but for all the comrades who had died and for those who had stood up for us, not knowing that their leader had betrayed them. Why couldn't Michael have taken the members of the left and I into his confidence? Why did he, after all these years, trust us so little? How did he plan to govern, given the harsh conditionalities that the IMF would exact? Was this man leading his followers to a place of liberation and self-respect? Who was this man and how many times had he lied to me before? In my heart of hearts, I knew that this revelation would have a devastating impact on our relationship. My two worlds had collided.

As a student of politics I felt I needed to do my own research on the IMF. In pursuit of this, I discovered a book by Cheryl

Payer, *The Debt Trap.* After reading it, I was so alarmed that I passed it on to D.K. Duncan. The book used several case studies to show the role and impact of IMF programmes in several countries, and how they ended up being caught in a 'debt trap' from which they could not escape. D.K. introduced the book to the party secretariat, and several copies were distributed within the party. Cheryl Payer was eventually invited to be the special guest of the party at the 1980 national executive council meeting.

Deep in my gut I knew that we were entering another phase of the struggle — a dangerous phase that could determine our success or failure. The escalating violence had not stopped us. Seaga had not stopped us. The US administration had not stopped us. The IMF would.

The IMF would become the nemesis of the People's National Party, and of the country, for decades to come.

The university group of Norman Girvan, Michael Witter, George Beckford and Louis Lindsay took up the challenge to find an alternative to the IMF. Within a period of three weeks — from the end of December through to January 1977 — they worked as they had never worked before. With the strongest possible support from D.K. Duncan and the newly created Ministry of National Mobilisation and Human Resource Development, the team received countless suggestions from people across Jamaica. The entire bureaucracy was set up to create an alternative production plan, one that would make the IMF irrelevant and redundant. When Michael first saw the plan, he turned quickly to the section on foreign exchange. Not satisfied that it had adequately addressed that critical issue, he knew it would have to be discarded. He found the section on foreign exchange idealistic, inadequate and unrealistic, and that was the end of the plan in that form. However, Michael did salvage elements of it so that the left wing would know that their work was not in vain. In the meantime, he had discussions with Prime Minister James Callaghan of Britain, and Prime Minister Pierre Elliott Trudeau of Canada about the harsh conditions that the IMF was demanding of Jamaica.

Discussions began to take place within the PNP around IMF conditionality and the universal nature of the IMF programmes with the same prescriptions for all countries. Was the IMF purely an economic institution set up after the World War II to assist Third World countries with balance of payment programmes? Or had it been set up to perpetuate the dominance and exploitation of countries on the periphery of international capitalism? The party took the latter view, and even as Jamaica entered into agreement after agreement with the IMF, the PNP tried to ensure that its members understood clearly the political role and impact of this US-controlled agency.

The Department of Government was dominated largely by members of the then Communist Workers Liberation League (WLL) who were critical of the PNP for being 'mouth-water' socialists. The PNP was like the meat in a sandwich with the JLP on top and the WLL beneath. It was not a comfortable position to be in. Michael continued to be under a great deal of stress and often felt frustrated and angry. On one occasion the head of the IMF delegation, in discussions with him, told him boldly that he, Michael was the problem. Later, we would see graffiti on the walls stating that IMF stood for, "It's Manley's fault".

Within the secretariat, our task was to ensure that the masses of the people understood that we were being punished for changing the power balance within Jamaica and throughout the world. As we passed legislation after legislation to ameliorate the conditions under which the majority lived, there was immediate reaction from the opposition and their allies. Michael spent much time travelling the world, espousing his thoughts on the state of injustice that existed between the so-called First World and the Third World. The PNP Women's Movement had established offices in the Secretariat, as well. Leaders in the Movement and a hardworking assistant, Pearl Earle, ably assisted me. These were hardworking and rewarding years. We took on the struggle against the IMF with courage and vigour, educating party members about what to expect. I stood up in the major party as an advocate on behalf of women. I was often criticized but I stood firm and always had the support of Michael, as Party Leader.

These messages were discussed at the level of the party newspaper, the *Rising Sun.* In addition to distributing information through traditional newspaper, radio and television advertisements, our political education programme developed the third week programme. In the third week of every month, a group of comrades, including a few members of parliament and professionals, were prepared by the secretariat and sent out simultaneously to all 60 constituencies to teach the political education lesson of the month. Topics included the nature of imperialism generally and, in particular, the role of US imperialism in Latin America and the Caribbean.

There was no doubt that the PNP had the capacity to organise in a way that the JLP did not. The political education programme became the critical vehicle through which the people would be kept informed of the party's doings. When party groups met, the lectures and presentations were exciting and to a large extent contrary to what was being printed in the press, in particular in the *Gleaner,* where the portrayal of the PNP and its leader was demonic. In fact a cluster of opinion writers for the Gleaner saw it as their mission to denigrate Michael and the PNP on an ongoing basis. Their impact was overwhelming.

Tensions between the two factions of the party escalated, and rumours suggested that the left wing, under the leadership of D.K. Duncan, wanted to overthrow Michael. These rumours were largely fuelled by the fact that a major role of the newly formed Ministry of Mobilisation was to ensure that government's policies and programmes were carried out. As minister, Duncan often had to confront his cabinet colleagues about why their ministries were not performing adequately. The result was ongoing conflict. I remember when the ministry was created in 1976 — at a time when I barely knew Duncan — and Shirley said to me, 'I wish I knew him. I would tell him that it is madness to take on a ministry that has him monitoring and evaluating his colleagues. It won't work and it will probably destroy him.' Neither of us felt we knew him well enough to pass this message on.

Later in 1977, after the annual conference and at the first meeting of the National Executive Council, D.K. resigned his position as minister and general secretary, but not as member of parliament. In his letter of resignation, read by one of his colleagues in the ministry, Norma Segre, he noted that his position had become untenable. One of the immediate impacts of his resignation was that the party, having lost the leader of the left, somehow had to convince itself and other progressives in the country that it was not now on a right-wing path. And so it happened that when Fidel Castro came to Jamaica later in 1977, the visit helped the party to retain its left-wing credibility.

Several left-wing dignitaries who visited Jamaica during the late 1970s boosted the party's left-wing image during its negotiations and agreements with the IMF and particularly during the subsequent period of D.K.'s absence. In many cases their speeches were militant, as in the case of Samora Machel of Mozambique, or statesmanlike, as in the case of Fidel Castro and Julius Nyerere.

My first impression of Samora Machel was that he was a short, dynamic figure who walked tall. He was immaculately dressed in typical African style, and travelled with a huge entourage. He was an army man, as was obvious from the moment he stepped off the plane. A charismatic speaker, he was clear about his revolutionary bona fides. At the time of his visit to Jamaica, Mozambique was embroiled in a civil war and was under severe pressure from the apartheid government of South Africa. The sound bite from his speech at the anti-imperialist rally held at the National Arena the following day stated it was necessary to 'kill the crocodile in the egg'. Many Jamaicans were chilled by this remark, though the ideological left to delight the militancy of his remarks. Before he left Jamaica, Governor General Glasspole awarded Machel the Order of Jamaica in recognition of his role as a critical symbol of the African Liberation Movement.

A week after Machel's arrival, Fidel Castro stepped onto Jamaican soil for the first time. Dressed in his usual olive-green army fatigues complete with military cap, he disembarked from a 200-foot brown and white training ship of the Cuban merchant fleet, the *Jose Marti,* named after the Cuban national hero. A 21-gun salute and crowds of admirers greeted him. The Governor General met him and officially introduced him to Michael and I. Members of the cabinet and of parliament were also in attendance. The JLP had announced earlier that it would boycott the visit and its members were true to their word. Leaders of the church community were also notably absent.

Keeping Fidel safe was the greatest challenge for the security forces and everything was put in place to ensure his safety. For example, he travelled with a large security detail, one of whom tasted his food. Jamaicans were never told where he slept at night. The Cuban reception was held on a Cuban sea vessel.

Fidel's arrival was watched with great suspicion by conservatives, but from the moment he arrived until his departure five days later, he took into account the sensitivity and complexity of Jamaica's two-party liberal democracy, holding to his principles but offending no one. Fidel was the supreme statesman who wanted to ensure that his visit would be helpful to his friend Michael, who he knew was in a dangerous political situation. He understood the courage behind Michael's invitation to Jamaica – a country he had long wanted to see. He used the opportunity to reiterate that Cuba would never interfere in Jamaican affairs, and he applauded the opposition Jamaica Labour Party, by showing his appreciation for the fact that they had not supported the US blockade of Cuba. While in full praise of Michael and his democratic socialist approach, Fidel made it clear to the left wing of the party that he would not wish the Cuban struggle on anyone, for it was a difficult one. He urged the left inside and outside of the party to support Michael and democratic socialism.

The highlight of Fidel's visit was a mass rally, 100,000 strong, held in Sam Sharpe Square. He, too, was awarded the Order of Jamaica for being a 'giant in the struggle against imperialism, intervention and aggression.' But the high point of his visit was personal. He visited our retreat in the Blue Mountains. There, he spoke of his love for Jamaica and how thrilled he was to be here at last. He stood on the mountaintop and looked across, as if looking at Cuba's Oriente Province, that westerly region of Cuba just 90 miles from Jamaica.

The back-to-back visits of Machel and Fidel went a long way towards assuring the left wing inside the party and the country that even with the departure of D.K. Duncan, the party had not moved away from its anti-imperialist position.

In the midst of all this there was a change of administration within the United States as Jimmy Carter came to power. Michael was overjoyed that a democrat now occupied the White House, and hoped that under the Carter administration, the relations between Jamaica and the United States would become less tense. But we overestimated what the president could do on his own.

I remember the morning we arrived in Washington for the official visit at the White House. As usual, Michael had travelled with his personal security officer, Barry Ford. But the moment we stepped off the plane and planted our feet on the tarmac, the US security forces took over. Michael was suddenly surrounded by at least 15 security men, all looking stern and communicating with each other through earphones and other electronic devices. I wondered how the president of the United States survived this — always being surrounded by security. We were soon whisked away in a limousine to our hotel suite. We remained largely inside the hotel because on the one occasion that we ventured out, our security attracted so much attention that we felt like fish in a bowl, trapped and, in spite of the security, vulnerable.

Because of the historic nature of the visit, we took two of the children, Sarah and Natasha, with us. Rachel as usual was travelling overseas, and Joseph was at boarding school. My sister Shirley had become a constant source of support to me on many of my overseas trips and she came along with her two children, Marguerite and Douglas. Her husband, Richard, was part of the official delegation as minister of state in the Ministry of Finance. The left wing in the party had become increasingly suspicious of young Fletcher as he was seen by them as someone more intent on 'balancing the books' than anything else, at the expense of the immediate needs of the masses. Little did we know how isolated Richard himself was in the Ministry of Finance.

We knew that the Carter team, unlike the Ford–Kissinger team that had preceded it, was open to what we were attempting in Jamaica. Several things were on our minds as we prepared for these official talks. We were already well established in an IMF programme, although the worst of its terms had been scaled down, thanks to the interventions of Callaghan and Trudeau. An IMF Net Domestic Assets test was pending, and earlier, as we left Jamaica, Finance Minister David Coore had assured us that we were able to meet all its conditions. The Jamaican government wanted President Carter to see that we were managing our economic affairs well and certainly passing the test would be evidence of this. We did not want to be embarrassed by news of a failed test while on an official visit to the White House. Interestingly, as he received us, the president commented on how well we were doing: that was his understanding of our situation. But our darkest fears were realised when Coore telephoned Michael to tell him that we had failed the IMF's test by a negligible margin. The IMF immediately suspended the standby agreement, under which only one payment to Jamaica had been made. Michael surmised that once again this would be taken by the United States as confirmation that we were incapable of managing the economy.

On returning to Jamaica, Michael would face yet another painful hurdle as he decided that because of the failure of the IMF test, he would have to replace Coore as finance minister. On a personal level, I cannot remember ever seeing him in so much agony. As a young boy of ten, when he first went to Jamaica College and was ostracised by his entire first-form class, David Coore had been the only boy who spoke to him. They had remained friends ever since. David's second wife Myrthe was my good friend and an active member of the Cabinet Wives' Association. We came from a similar class background and she used to say to me that no one expected women like us to reach the level we had reached, and that we should never, ever leave our marriages.

During our White House visit, little did we know that the topic of Cuba would be first on the agenda and would take up considerable time in the deliberations. The president wanted to know why we supported Cuba. I could see Michael taking a deep breath before answering this oft-repeated question. He talked about our non-aligned foreign policy and the fact that Cuba was our nearest neighbour, and about the close ties between Jamaica and Cuba over the years, dating from the time of slavery. He pointed out that although he was anti-communist, he believed that communist countries had a right to their ideology, but assured the president that there was no possibility of Jamaica becoming communist. Michael took the opportunity to plead with him to use his good offices to end the embargo against Cuba. Cyrus Vance, secretary of state, Zbigniew Brzezinski and Andrew Young were among those at the official talks. In spite of the goodwill of the president, we came away knowing that we had not convinced him and his team about the reasons for our friendship with Fidel.

Michael announced in March of 1980 that elections would be held as soon as the Electoral Advisory Committee informed him that everything was in place. The months leading up to those elections would be some of the toughest we would go through as we waited for the committee to give the go-ahead. The die was cast. Everything was in place for a PNP defeat. From the perspective of the cold war, true to form, there was unanimity between elements in the US administration and leadership elements within both our party and the opposing one. They wanted us out. It was not surprising that after a tumultuous year, Michael called the election nine months early.

A long election campaign typically creates a period of uncertainty. This one was no exception. Michael and Seaga squared off like boxers in a ring. Communication between them was non-existent. The PNP was at its highest level of organisation and development ever, particularly through the Canvassers Training Programme and the Political Education Programme. The right wing inside and outside of the PNP was pulling together. The left wing inside and outside of the PNP was pulling together. Everywhere there was war. In their fear of communism, Jamaicans of the middle class, many of whom had supported us in 1972, were leaving in droves, mainly for the United States. Many who left came back on Election Day to vote us out, to 'save Jamaica' from a communist fate. Organisations such as the recently-formed PSOJ were making their presence felt as they lashed out at what they saw as the government's inept economic policies and empty political rhetoric.

The 1980 election would be the bloodiest in Jamaica's history. By Election Day it was estimated that hundreds of people had been killed and untold numbers injured. Among many tragic incidents was the murder of Roy McGann, MP for East Rural St Andrew, and his bodyguard, Acting Corporal Errol White in Gordon Town, on the outskirts of St Andrew. Elsewhere, gunmen shot seven people on National Heroes Day. Two children were killed in Top Hill, St Elizabeth, where PNP and JLP supporters clashed. Gunfire disrupted a PNP rally in Spanish Town, where D.K. Duncan was seen defending himself with his licensed firearm. The incident was broadcast over public television. The country seemed to have gone mad.

In the middle of all of this turmoil, I had gone to the gynaecologist to get my tubes tied. Michael had always wanted more children, while I was happy with one. So imagine my surprise, when in the doctor's office, ready and wearing the smock, I suddenly changed my mind. I decided that it was time to try for a son. Michael was thrilled when I called him with the news, and within a month I found out I was pregnant.

Late on October 30, 1980, Election Day, Michael and I waited at home at Washington Close for the results. As usual, Michael went to bed as soon as the polls closed. I was busy with little David, born prematurely three months earlier, weighing only two pounds eight ounces. The most distressing year of my life was coming to a close. There was no doubt in my mind that we would lose the elections. I had told Michael this many times when he telephoned me from the campaign trail. He would describe the crowds and their enthusiasm, and I would respond by describing what I had heard when I visited David several times a day where he lay in an incubator in the special ward at the University Hospital.

There, as I fed him milk expressed from my breast (a process I hated because I smelled constantly of milk), I would speak to other mothers of premature babies, women whom I felt I knew because they were the people on whose behalf I had fought so relentlessly throughout the past decade, women who wanted their voices to be heard, women who wanted to be valued for the silent, challenging and selfless roles they were playing in bringing up children, often without men. Women like my mother, who created something from nothing and whose only task in life was to ensure that their children had an education and therefore a chance to get on in life; women struggling to survive, economically and psychologically.

We talked of many things as we waited to visit our babies. Already we had a natural bond. We were worried about how we would cope with these small babies if they lived. Some of the women would not be able to breastfeed — what would they do without baby formula, which was one of the items not available in Jamaica at the time? But conversations quickly turned to the political situation. Some wanted to know and understand more clearly what was happening in Jamaica. Why was there so much hostility to what the People's National Party was doing? Some of them just wanted peace and were tired of the ideological battles. They were tired of tribal conflict between the two warring parties. Others wanted to know why the PNP was so much against the United States, a place to which, if given half a chance, they would wish to go. Some wanted foreign goods, such as American apples, on the shelves even if they couldn't afford to buy them. Most just wanted to be able to get food for their children.

What was most striking was that they said they wanted Michael to live, and some of them felt that if the PNP won the elections, the communists outside the party, who they perceived as the communists within, would stage a 'takeover' and get rid of him. These discussions left me quite shaken.

Three weeks later, the doctors were satisfied that the best thing now was for David to be at home. The very morning we took him home, Roy McGann's body was brought to the hospital. PNP supporters and others who had heard of the murder, or were with Roy when he was killed, were already assembling there. There was tension in the air. This was the first time that a member of parliament had been murdered. Michael and I wanted to be with the people, but we were both clear that David had to be our first priority. Roy had died. David was struggling to live. Uppermost in our minds was getting our tiny, fragile baby out of there. I covered him up as best I could and Michael's security team hurried us out. No one had seen or recognised us.

The night of the election, my breasts ached more then ever from the concentration of milk. I had to keep expressing it. Anticipating this day, I had made contingency plans with Roma to send me baby formula from the United States in case I got separated from David for any length of time. I had also made arrangements with Barclay Ewart that, depending on what happened, I would telephone him and say I was 'sending up the champagne'. This was a code indicating that I was sending the two children accompanied by Nurse. I chose Barclay because he was a businessman and I felt that although he was known as a close friend of Michael's, no one would get in the way of anything he did.

By the time the 1980 election came around, we had been living in our private home at Washington Close for about 2 years. Jamaica House had become more and more a public space, and we felt the need to escape. Washington close was now packed with people, as it often had been over the years, and I was kept busy serving people food and drinks, and feeding the baby. It must have been 7:00 p.m. when I answered the telephone and Arnold Bertram, MP for N.E. St Ann, told me in an agitated voice that the boxes pouring into Brown's Town from all over his constituency had majority votes for the Jamaica Labour Party. If this was happening in N.E. St Ann, a traditional PNP stronghold, there was no doubt in his mind that the PNP would be wiped out. I woke Michael and he spoke to Arnold. Their exchange seemed to confirm that we had lost. In fact as we watched the seat count unfold on television, we soon realised that the JLP, under the leadership of Seaga, had won decisively. The PNP was left with a mere nine of the 60 seats. The JLP had got 58 per cent of the votes and the PNP a mere 41 per cent.

Although I had not expected that we would win, I was shocked at the extent of the defeat. In spite of this, 350,000 persons of a voting population of almost one million had voted for us. I was immediately worried about the impact the Seaga victory would have on the party and on us personally. The middle classes began celebrating what they perceived as a 'turning back', not only of democratic socialism, but of communism.

An atmosphere of fear had been growing ever since the election victory in 1976. Now it was fully fledged. We immediately began to think through our options in order to keep safe. We were convinced that the CIA, in collaboration with Seaga, would be coming after us.

D.K. Duncan, now general secretary and a lightning rod for the party, had had great difficulty getting in from South St Elizabeth the night before. He had telephoned to say the security forces were harassing him and was not sure he would make it to Kingston alive. On the night before election night, and on the day of the election itself, reports like this flooded in from across the country — news of comrades being harassed by the security forces and the JLP. Comrades, in turn, were concerned about the safety of their leader. On election day Michael warned D.K. that 'they', by which he meant the Labourite followers of the opposition, the JLP itself and the security forces, were out to get him and that he should stay home. So Duncan left home only once to visit his constituency and to vote. He had a safe urban constituency, East Central St Andrew, and had been working in the countryside assisting other constituencies.

I had always heard stories about the Jamaica Labour Party. When I thought of Seaga I thought of Tivoli Gardens, a section of the West Kingston constituency, which he represented. The impression we had was of a community of hard-core gunmen who were under Seaga's highly centralised control. These were men he could call on and send out to assist Labourites in their constituencies who might be in any kind of trouble. My perception of him was of a hard, cold person capable of doing anything that the CIA and the Americans wanted, and more.

Following the election results, the house at Washington Close was like a funeral home. People moved around aimlessly, not quite knowing what to do or where to go. We were broken. We knew the dream had been deferred and would be difficult to rebuild. But for now, we were concerned for our safety and the safety of those around us. The plight of the masses of the people who had stood up for socialism concerned us. We knew that, in many cases, they would become refugees in their own land. Many would have to flee their homeland in the dead of night; some would be harmed physically and emotionally. Above all, they would be unsure of their future and that of their beloved leader. We would never know the extent of their pain and hurt. We would never know their sense of loss of home and family and of the struggle. What we knew for sure, was that many of our comrades would experience victimisation at the hands of Labourites, whose time had now come.

Michael sent for his mother. At times of crisis, she was always there for him, and he always sought her advice, even if he sometimes ignored it. As he and I sat together, feeling alone in the world, his mother floated into the room. We both stood as she embraced us together in one giant hug, telling us it was all right and that this, too, would pass. Mardi knew what political defeat was like.

At times like these, Mardi simply took over. Foremost in her mind was her son's happiness. It always worried her that Michael tended to be reckless, for example, in announcing programmes that the party was not ready for, such as the relationship with Fidel and Cuba, or travelling on Fidel's private plane to a non-aligned conference in Cuba. He was also reckless in his private life. There were times when he could not be stopped. It was as though there was a devil inside him. She cautioned us not to do anything rash, such as going into exile in Cuba. She took me aside and reminded me that Norman too had been stubborn and that although she and others had advised him not to hold the referendum on whether or not Jamaica should stay in the West Indian Federation, he had gone ahead with it. The loss of the referendum and the subsequent loss of the elections had broken his heart. She felt that he never recovered. Michael was now 56 years old, and Mardi did not want this election defeat to break her son's heart.

We stayed together that night — mother, son and daughter-in-law — determined to face the odds. Comrades came and went like shadows in the night, each preoccupied with his own safety. I remember wishing that I knew how to pray, how to ask for God's guidance. I couldn't remember how. It had been a long time since I had talked to God.

From the start, Michael and I had had differences on the subject of religion. Though brought up in the fundamentalist Brethren Church, I had studied Marxism, and over time, I had begun to question my Christian faith. Michael thought of God as someone to whom he felt close when he went to Nyumbani and lay on the ground, gazing up at the sky through the trees. He was terribly embarrassed when comrades sang to him the hymn 'I Must Have the Saviour with Me'. He was self-conscious over references they made to Joshua in the Bible breaking down the barriers of the city. It was an image he would put up with for the benefit of the party. He knew the comrades meant well.

It is difficult to explain why, despite Michael's insistence that I stay home with Natasha and David, and despite the perceived danger, I knew that I would not leave his side. Certain situations are the very context of one's life, beyond fear. In a way, all that Michael and I had lived through, all our principles and what we stood for, were embodied in the reality of that evening. I had to face it all and see it through; not to have done so would have been as impossible as avoiding death. Defeat in this case was part of the context of living so intensely as an architect of those eight years and their meaning, for better or worse. Whatever happened to me that night, it was our destiny. I knew I couldn't run from that.

As we took to the streets on our way to PNP headquarters where Duncan and others were holding a press conference,

Michael was greeted with positive vibes from many citizens who were out that night. People shouted to him to continue the fight, not to be disheartened, that they still loved him and were grateful for what he had done on their behalf. Later that night we drove up to the Ewarts' home to collect Nurse and the children. As we drove around the city, we were amazed at the reception we got from the crowds. There was no doubt in our minds that the people still adored Michael. Many had in fact voted against the PNP because they believed this would save him — from the left wing, from the Americans.

When we arrived at last at the press conference taking place at PNP headquarters, we felt that we had come home. Whatever happened, Michael's ongoing popularity would help to keep us safe. Later we returned to Washington Close with the children, feeling glad to be alive, but knowing we faced an uncertain future.

Chapter 9

When we woke the next morning, my overwhelming feeling was one of relief — of a huge burden having been lifted from my shoulders. I looked across the bed at my husband, who was determined to put on his best face. He just sighed. We held each other for a while, saying nothing. The night had passed and we were happy to be safe. The house had finally settled down after the bad news of the defeat. Nothing moved. The children were still asleep. David would sleep late as usual. I had grown accustomed to having so many people around me — comrades and friends. But now there was a sense of emptiness, a sense of loss not just of the election, but even more so, of self, of the struggle. As I cuddled Michael in my arms like a mother soothing a hurt child, I began to wonder what it was all about and why I felt so confused.

What would this new regime under Seaga be like?

I thought of those who had died. I thought too of the many party members who had worked so tirelessly for a dream in which they believed. They had believed that something more was possible for Jamaica as a place of social justice, equality, dignity and pride — a place where women and men respected each other. The struggle had consumed us. We had been obsessed with it. Many of us had mortgaged our homes for the struggle. Many of us were broke, as Michael and I were.

We had the house we lived in, that was all. We had nothing to sell. This was not a new experience for Michael, as he had watched his father wrestle with political debts, selling Drumblair and buying it back again, and much later, after retirement, having to rent his home in Kingston to live at his Blue Mountain cottage, Nomdmi. I thought of our international friends who supported the idea of a third path for countries like ours. During the day I knew that telephone calls would come from leaders in the Caribbean and elsewhere in the world. I remember thinking about the children, including Joseph and Della, his wife, who were in Cuba. They would know by now. I thought of Rachel who was living in Barbados and Sarah in high school in Kingston. And then I thought of the two little ones, Natasha, six, and David, three months old. At least he was out of the hospital. How would this defeat affect them? I was sure that the younger ones would suffer in school even more now than before. Being a Manley in the 1970s was often difficult for the children. Being the child of any public face in the party was difficult.

Soon the telephones began to ring. We phoned Edward Seaga and congratulated him, informing him that we would depart Jamaica House, where we still had our offices, as soon as possible. To our surprise, Mr Seaga was kind and thoughtful and assured Michael that everything would be done to make the transition easy for him, including allowing him to keep his security personnel for as long as he wished. I spoke to him also and requested that my security woman, Rosalie McDonald, who had been assigned to me since 1974, stay on. What a surprise we got! We had expected to be killed or locked up, but Michael was as popular as ever. Attempting to harm or muzzle him might have caused a civil war and Seaga obviously knew that.

Rosie and Nurse Brown, Natasha's nanny, encouraged us by quoting scripture verses and telling us to have faith. They knew they couldn't say this to 'Mr Mike', but I listened to them and was grateful for their ongoing love and support.

Everything outside looked the same, as if nothing had happened. I decided to do something that I had been unable to do all those years. I started to clean the house. While Michael took telephone calls, I gave the kitchen a good spring-cleaning. Rosie helped me and then later on her sister Ruby came and stayed for a while until we sorted out our household staff and other arrangements. Michael and I longed for the solace of Nyumbani. Mardi used to say the hills were a place of healing and that had also been our experience. But it would have to wait. There was too much uncertainty in our lives, too many things to do.

Michael did his best to face a life of politics in opposition, but he was beginning to have grave doubts about his leadership and had to be constantly reassured. I worried about him because, like his father, he took things too personally. Already he was beginning to say this was entirely his fault. He was thinking of offering to resign. But most of all he needed a break. He felt weighed down. He had become the beating stick for so many things and he was tired, so tired. Mardi and I worried about him. She had seen it all before with Norman — not winning his seat in 1944 and later losing the elections in 1962. But it was the loss of the referendum that had defeated him in life, a loss from which he had never recovered. Everything had to be done to ensure that Michael was not defeated personally by this loss.

We had known that our chances of winning were slim. We had known that calling the elections early was the correct decision for a government that had lost its legitimacy. Hitting the road for the 'Gone clear' tour across Jamaica and seeing the thousands of people who came out to greet Michael and the PNP team, perhaps those campaigning felt that victory was possible. It was different for me. Because of David I was unable to campaign the way I usually would. But I did get a chance to talk to the masses of the people on a one-to-one basis, particularly to new mothers at the University Hospital. They were very clear. They loved Michael Manley but they would vote him out in order to protect him, to save his life. If he won, they said, either the left wing, inside or outside the party, would get him; and if they didn't, the Americans would. In any case they were tired of the suffering — the shortages of food and basic items such as soap and sanitary napkins, and the hostility they had to put up with from the Labourites in their communities.

Michael went into a deep, reflective mood that lasted for some time. He did not know how he would make a living. I had not been allowed to work for pay for the entire decade of the 1970s. We had no money. The situation looked desperate. We were both on the verge of a nervous breakdown without knowing it. This manifested itself differently in him and in me, each going through fundamental changes and, at the same time, each trying to help the other. I was marginally aware of Michael's trauma, but foremost in my mind was David, and the uncertainty of whether he would live. I didn't have time to think about the happenings of the party, and therefore, where Michael would go next.

Within two days of the election, Seaga was sworn in as prime minister, and a few days after that, he expelled the Cuban ambassador to Jamaica, Ulises Estrada, and severed ties with Cuba as he began to rebuild relations with the United States.

A group of us, including Portia Simpson and D.K., returned to the secretariat immediately; our reaction was to begin the rebuilding process. The most critical thing was to get in touch with comrades to ensure that they were coping and then to get down to the business of assessing what had happened.

As I evaluated the political process of the 1970s, I found myself also examining my personal relationship with Michael. I began to see how different we were, particularly in defeat. Where I came from, you took your licks and moved on. My mother had no time for self-pity. Michael withdrew into himself and began a process of self-flagellation. He needed to be bolstered continually. Suddenly I found that I no longer had tolerance for this aspect of his personality. In the past I would have arranged for his favourite people to visit and cheer him up. I had no desire now to do this. His insecurity and self-involvement had reached a level that was astonishing to me. It seemed to represent such weakness.

Within a year of David's birth, I realised that I was losing interest in my marriage. I didn't recognise Michael any more. Even in party meetings it was as if a part of him had died, and in private it was clear that he was hurting deeply. He decided to get out of Jamaica to his favourite city, London, a place that always seemed to put everything right for him. He tried to make this trip at least once a year, escaping to a big city where he was largely anonymous and where he could do simple things like buy a newspaper on the street or go into a butcher's shop. On this trip, which took place a short time after the election defeat of 1980, he did not want me to come with him. He wanted to be alone, he said. I didn't believe he would be alone, I knew him too well for that. It occurred to me then that perhaps he too was evaluating the marriage, although he would later deny this. Soon he began travelling to the United States to make a living lecturing and was away a great deal. It made no economic sense for me to accompany him. For a couple who had been so intimately involved, we were now, for the first time since we met, spending a great deal of time away from each other.

Gradually I began to suspect that he was having an affair with a married woman on the periphery of our group of friends. I threatened him, saying that if he was having an affair with her, I would leave him. I'm not sure why, but for me this was the last straw. We had had heated discussions in the past about his affairs, and the condition for my staying with him was that he would no longer have affairs with women in our immediate circle. He assured me now that he had no interest in this woman. But one day I answered our home phone, which we kept for calls only to each other, and she was on the other end. I was shocked. She mumbled something about needing advice on Roses. With proof that he was having the affair, I stopped being committed to my marriage. I knew it was only a matter of time before I left, and I told him so. He didn't take me seriously. In his entire life, he told me, no woman had ever left him.

Fortunately, I had a lot of time on my hands and got even more involved in the rebuilding of the party. As this work continued, I spent a great deal of time with Natasha and David

— something that had previously been near impossible for me to do. The children kept me going. I had little or no social life. We were invited to few public functions and it took courage to be with people, particularly those we knew didn't support us and who were celebrating our loss.

Soon, what I perceived as Michael's reform began. This came about at the same time I was reassessing my marriage. A different set of people would visit Michael at Washington Close, including some from the private sector and the party's right wing. Michael's popularity among the masses continued to be huge but he yearned to be loved by his own social class again, as he had been in 1972 before ideology took over the party, the way things had been during the Camelot years when he could do no wrong, when it seemed all of Jamaica supported him and the PNP. As a popular song put it at the time, it was 'the dawning of a brand new day' and they had all joined to 'hail the man'. He yearned for that feeling again. Later, in a speech to the PNP annual conference, he would state that he wanted 'no quarrel', not with the factions within the party, nor with the wider society.

The loss of the election was one thing. That didn't faze me. What really concerned me was the future of the wider movement for change. Was this 'a dream deferred', to use the Langston Hughes phrase, or was the dream dead?

I was in the middle of research for my master's and wanted to do a PhD. I felt this was the time to begin to think of my two young children and myself. Michael and I talked about it. I shared with him how I was feeling about our marriage: how empty, how excluded by him I felt for the first time since we had met. He seemed to put up a protective wall around himself so that no one could see his personal hurt and his despair. He was like a zombie. And so throughout 1981 he wandered alone. I felt left out of his life, and spent most of my time either on the UWI campus or alone at home. I also looked to Marxism, the early Marx, to see to what extent dialectical methodology could help me understand the process Jamaican politics had just gone through. It helped, but not nearly enough. I knew the marriage was over, and that already he was intensifying his latest affair. I too was in the process of falling in love.

I enjoyed working with D.K., and was amazed at how he, in contrast to Michael, handled the electoral defeat. He did not take it personally. He said that he and Michael had discussed several times that a defeat was highly possible but that what was important was preserving the integrity of the movement. I began to admire this in him. He was shorter than Michael, and darker in complexion. He was younger than Michael by 16 years, and slim with an Afro and a beard — the beard made his face appear long and pointed and rather revolutionary-looking, I thought. He always wore a cap or tam. We grew closer, and before I knew it we were falling hopelessly in love. D.K. told me that 12 years earlier he had seen me in a television advertisement on JBC and knew that one day we would be together. When he got involved with the PNP, I was already Michael's wife, and D.K. recognised that the goal of democratic socialism was bigger than any individual. I was critical to this process if Michael was to succeed. Once Michael turned his back on the struggle, however, there was no longer any need for D.K. to keep his feelings secret.

I was confused and needed a relationship that would guide me. D.K. provided that love and clarity. He did not break up my marriage. He came into my life at a time when I knew I could no longer deal with Michael's infidelities, a time when I could no longer deal with the strictures of being Mrs Michael Manley, a time when Michael's age — 17 years my senior — was beginning to be a problem for me. Suddenly he looked and acted so old. I was lonely and needed to throw off all the constraints and shackles of public life and just be reckless — if only for a while. D.K. and I made arrangements to meet every day. We delighted in each other. We were still involved in party meetings. We assessed the situation over and over again, knowing we were being irresponsible and reckless — and yet we couldn't help ourselves. The impact of our relationship on the party was immediate, and their response understandably alarmed. I wondered if this might have been different if his affair had been as public as mine.

It was inevitable that Michael should find out. Someone wrote him an anonymous letter detailing our affair, even revealing the house where we would meet. When I came home from the PNP secretariat one day in 1982, he called me into the bedroom for one of our talks. I knew it was serious because I noticed the way his jaw was twitching and how he was trying to control himself. He took the letter out of his pocket. He began to read: 'Comrade Leader, you need to know that your wife and Comrade Duncan' I stopped him and pleaded with him not to read any more. I confessed immediately and told Michael the truth: that I had fallen in love with D.K. and that he had become my life. I told him how burdensome it had

Beverley, Winnie Mandela and Dessima Williams in Massachusetts

Beverley and Nancy Wilson

Beverley as the Jamaican representative to the U.N. Commission on the status of Women, Vienna, Austria

Beverley and Tony Abrahams on The Breakfast Club

David, Beverley and Natasha at Michael's funeral

Beverley with Harry and Julia Belafonte, on The Breakfast Club

Beverley, with Jeanette Hutchinson and her sister, Lilleth, receiving the Pelican Award in 2000

Beverley and PJ, examining the Rod of Correction

Sisters Shirley, Roma and Beverley in 2006

Beverley and DK

The five Manley Children: (standing) Joseph and Rachel, with Natasha, David and Sarah

David and Natasha in 2006

been for me not to tell him and that I was actually relieved that he had found out. By this time we were both in tears. I reached for my suitcase high on top of the clothes cupboard. He asked what I was doing. I told him that I was leaving, that I would go to my mother's. I knew this would be hell for me but I had nowhere else to go. Michael took the suitcase from me and told me that I wasn't going anywhere, that we would work it out. His response surprised me — I knew how much he was hurting. As we lay in bed that night, he held me in his arms. He fell asleep quickly, while I lay awake for some time, confused by his reaction, wondering what was next.

The following day he said that if I felt I had to continue with the affair, he would ask only that I stop meeting at the same place and that I be as discreet as possible until I got over it, for he knew I would get over it. An affair, he said, was hardly a reason to end a marriage. Whatever I had to sort out, he hoped I could sort it out within our relationship. He didn't want any more marriages. He had already made up his mind to grow old with me.

And so the affair continued. Michael's approach did not have the effect he had intended. The more I got to know D.K., the more I was sure that I wanted to spend the rest of my life with him. Michael tried everything, including inviting certain party members to talk to me. He even arranged for Freddie Hickling, a psychiatrist and later a member of the Participatory Research Group, to come to the house to find out why I was leaving him. I will always remember Freddie's parting words: 'I do not fret for you. You are obviously a woman of power to be having a relationship with the party leader and his general secretary at the same time.' Freddie saw my relationships as part of a power struggle. I was shocked that I myself had not seen them that way.

In 1983 I moved into a two-bedroom flat at the back of my mother's house that had become vacant around that time. She had built a flat on either side of her main house — the one she had bought with money saved during her marriage — in the event that if any man ever took advantage of her girl-children, they would have a place to come home to. Michael and I would still see each other, and even go jogging together. We did not yet consider the marriage at an end.

My mother couldn't believe that Michael and I were separating. From all she could see we had a good marriage. The only thing she knew was that Michael had an insanely jealous streak. For example, if I had an appointment in a rural area and didn't return home when I was expected, he would telephone her several times to find out if she had heard from me. And besides, for her, marriage, despite all its hills and valleys, was 'till death do us part'. I should follow her example, she said, stay and make the marriage work. I told her that I felt I would die if I stayed. She agreed to let me live with her on the condition that it was just 'a break' from my marriage. After all, she said, I had been through a great deal, a premature baby and the loss of the elections, all in one year. She then went on to mutter that she had warned me about marrying a man who had been married three times before; something had to be wrong with him. I reminded her that because of the sacrifices her generation of women had been willing to make, my generation had choices that hers did not have. I was choosing to leave, and to live.

I decided not to say anything to Rachel, who was living in Barbados at the time. I talked about our situation to Joseph and his wife Della, who had recently returned from Cuba where they had both attended university. They were staying in our home until they settled down and found their own place. I was happy for this, as I was concerned about Michael being on his own. He was hurting so much. Jo and Della told me they would take care of him. Rosie stayed on with him and became his right-hand person. I knew I was leaving him well cared for. Sarah was also living with us, so she knew what was happening, but she was preoccupied with her own teenage rebellion. At an appropriate time I would tell Natasha, but not before I was absolutely sure that I would not be going back. As long as the children were there, Nurse would be there to protect them. They were like her babies.

Several years passed before Rachel forgave me for not telling her what was happening in the marriage. But I was going through so much turmoil that I just wanted privacy. As ever, it was my sisters, both living overseas, in whom I confided.

Michael was his usual courteous self, ensuring that I was as comfortable as possible in the flat. He said that as long as I was there, he would consider me his wife and I could come and go from our marital home as I pleased. If it needed to be made more comfortable he would make the necessary arrangements. However, the minute I decided to leave the flat and get my own place, he said, the marriage would be over. I agreed.

At the outset, the children stayed with him during the week and came to me on weekends, but I soon realised that, in my desperation, I had jumped from the frying pan into the fire. It was terrible for them at Mama's. She criticised everything they did. Also, I couldn't see D.K. at my mother's house. I sneaked him in one night and she was abusive to him. I couldn't have any visitors at all. Mama would present herself at my door and do everything she could to embarrass me. My brother's teenage son, Mark, was living with her at the time and she quarrelled with him constantly. Once again, I was waking up to the sound of my mother's complaining voice. She beat Mark with anything that was available. I knew I had to find a place of my own.

For a while I lived between the two homes — Michael's and my mother's — and at Christmas 1982, when Rachel was home, Michael asked me if I would move back in. I refused, though I still wasn't ready to make the final break. I always said that when I moved my clothes, it would mean I was leaving forever.

During our long separation, Michael and I made numerous attempts to save our marriage. The children and I often spent time in Washington at Shirley's house, and on one of these occasions Michael came to see me. We left the children at Shirley's and went to a motel to talk things through once again. I remember him pleading with me to understand that he would do anything to save the marriage. If and when he got the chance to run the country again, he said, Jamaicans would see a new Michael Manley. I reminded him that when we first met, he had said that he would do only two terms in office. His reply was that at times during the 1970s he had thought of resigning but things had always taken a different turn. Now he looked forward to being in office again but not in the same way as before. He wanted history to remember him as someone who genuinely tried to make the lives of the marginalised masses better. In particular, I think it was important to him to be remembered highly by members of his own social class, many of whom felt he had deserted them. He believed that if he could find a way to continue on his chosen political path, it would have a positive impact on our marriage. But I knew that he had no more to give. He kept saying, 'I can't do this any more. I can't stand the conflict. I can't stand the personal attacks on me. I just can't do this any more.' We hugged each other and cried that night, knowing there was no future for us as a couple. Irreconcilable differences over ideology would be the real cause of the demise of our marriage.

About a year after I moved out of Washington Close, I returned for the last time to retrieve my clothes and make the break permanent. I remember that we were standing on the steps leading to the kitchen when Michael uttered the words 'You will never make it without me.' I was very conscious in that moment of all I had contributed to him, his family and the People's National Party, and I reminded him of this.

As he looked down on me, his thin lips trembling in outrage, I thought of the women across the centuries who had taken powerful decisions about their own lives. I knew there was a price to pay for what I was doing, but I had to escape from the shadow of this man who had dominated my life from the moment we met. I had to.

In the weeks and months that followed, his parting words echoed in my mind, and the more I thought about them, the more defiant I became — and confident. I had the rest of my life to live, and I *would* make it on my own.

Chapter 10

I resigned from the PNP Women's Movement in 1982, not so much because I had left my marriage but because I no longer felt that the PNP was the vehicle for the kind of fundamental change that Jamaica needed. I also believed that, in spite of all the successes of the PNP Women's Movement as the arm of a tribal political party, the time had come for a women's movement that could transcend partisan political lines. Later, D.K. would resign as general secretary after Michael was told that because of D.K.'s leftist ideology, the private sector would not fund the PNP. Michael also took the opportunity to ask him to end his relationship with me. D.K. had agreed to the former but would not agree to the latter. Michael was not surprised.

It was time now to move out of Mama's flat, and so I began to look for a town house to buy. Michael and I agreed that he would stay at Washington Close and that he would buy my half of the house so that I could buy a place where Natasha and David, who were now eight and two respectively, could live with me. I settled on a town house on Hopefield Avenue. It wasn't my first choice but it was what I could afford. I allowed Michael and his lawyers to do what was necessary and accepted the evaluation he gave me. I was very naïve about legal matters and about protecting myself, although I had been a crusader for the rights of women all my life. Up until that time there were no property laws that protected women. Later I would fight for these laws, which took almost a decade to be enacted. About ten years later, I remember sitting next to Prime Minister P.J. Patterson at a meeting and hearing him talk about the proposed property law. I couldn't resist sending him a facetious note, asking him to make it retroactive.

In the meantime, I continued to be concerned about where the party had gone wrong. I was not alone. A group of us from the working left formed the Participatory Research Group (PRG) to attempt to answer the question: Had the PNP been derailed by right-wing forces within the party and in the United States? In other words, had it been intentionally destabilised on its course of fundamental change? The group met for the next four years. The conceptualisation for the research and the discussions took place at my home on Hopefield Avenue. Then the meetings shifted to the home of Drs Winston and Sonia Davidson. Dr 'Winty' Davidson had been a local government councillor in the constituency of South St Andrew where Anthony Spaulding was member of parliament. Throughout all this time 'Winty' had remained my medical doctor, counsellor and friend. He was also a junior minister in the Ministry of Health in the 1970s and a specialist in community health. My master's thesis on the modern political period in Jamaica and the founding of the PNP was of critical importance in understanding the nature of the party. The group soon recognised that to get a better understanding of the Jamaican process, we had to go all the way back to 1492, when Columbus first saw Jamaica. The PNP had never been on track. The tribal nature of Jamaican two-party politics was not in the best interest of the country and, in order to move forward, both parties would have to be prepared to make significant changes. Unfortunately, the results of the research were never published.

While the PRG was active, I continued to fix up the Hopefield town house to turn it into a real home for the children. But I completely underestimated how challenging my life would be. For years D.K. lived with his wife for half of the week and with me for the other half. In the end, I decided that I had made a mistake and that I needed to get out of the relationship. I had just taken it for granted that we would both get divorced and marry. It hadn't turned out that way.

In the summer of 1986, with the help of Dr Hilbourne Watson, a left-wing Barbadian professor at Howard University in Washington, I was granted a two-year fellowship to begin the process for my PhD. Although Michael and I had not yet divorced, our marriage was over. I was isolated from the PNP, a process that had begun with my leaving Michael, and had progressed through the affair with D.K. and my departure from the PNP Women's Movement. Now I was isolated from those in society who felt that I had betrayed Michael. Michael had wanted us to work things out, and had told me that what I had done was embarrassing to him privately and publicly. At the time he wanted nothing more to do with me. Studying had always helped me to maintain a sense of self. And so I told Michael I was leaving the relationship with D.K. and going abroad, but that I could only do so if he committed to taking care of the children full time. He agreed, saying that with the help of Rosie and Nurse, he knew it was possible. He was so relieved to know I was leaving D.K. that he was willing to do anything to help me. I wasn't entirely honest with D.K. I didn't tell him that this was about leaving him; I emphasised my desire to complete my PhD.

I rented out the Hopefield Avenue house and with that income plus the fellowship, I was sure I would be able to live reasonably well in Washington. Natasha was 11 and David was five, and Hopefield Avenue was the home that David had known. Leaving Jamaica was awful. It was difficult for both children, and I felt like a bad mother, but my pain was unbearable. I had to go.

Of course I visited home several times during the two years that I was away, and whenever I was in Jamaica my cousin, Jeanette Hutchinson and her daughter Racquel-Leigh, shared her home with us. On other occasions the children would come to see me in Washington. I remember one Christmas when they came and we bought a Christmas tree and celebrated in my flat. David, who was in preparatory school at Priory, was so excited to be with me. I took them to the airport to send them back home and as soon as they were out of sight, I broke down. I just stood there in that public space and cried. I cried for the failure of my marriage, for the failure of the relationship with D.K., and for all the bad choices I had made. I cried because when David had started to get upset at leaving me behind, Natasha had assumed the demeanour of an adult, held him by the hand, whispered something in his ear and then marched triumphantly onto the plane, dragging him along, never looking back.

During my time in Washington, D.K. often visited me, sometimes without warning. Sometimes I would come home from school and see him waiting at my door. While I was out of the apartment he would organise my papers and ensure that my refrigerator was full. We soon got back together. I delighted in my study programme at Howard and the course work that led to my PhD. I was assigned first of all to Dr Hilbourne Watson, who among other things taught a course on Greek civilization, and then to a Jamaican professor, Dr Dorith Grant Wisdom, who remains my close friend to this day. It was wonderful having their academic guidance and friendship. My two majors were Political Theory and Research Methodology. During this time I could feel my mind opening up. I particularly liked studying philosophy and this helped to place in some context what we had tried to do in Jamaica. After all, for centuries philosophers had asked questions about the 'common good' and about the best way to organise a society to this end. We, the PNP, had tried and failed.

I had other support. My two closest friends were Robert Ansah, from Ghana, and his wife Grace, from Jamaica. I often spent nights at their house and felt less lonely there. I would never have completed Research Methodology without the assistance of another Jamaican graduate student, Fern Johnson. I also came to know the interesting sections of D.C., such as Georgia Avenue where it was possible to go to a Jamaican nightclub and see Jamaicans and African Americans dancing with Red Stripe beer in hand and a rag in their back pocket. I hung out with African Americans for the first time, and got to know them. Sometimes I felt so caught up in the atmosphere there, that it was only when I re-entered the outside world that I remembered that I was in the United States.

Shirley and her husband Richard were also wonderfully supportive. Initially, my plan had been to stay with them in Washington, but I decided instead to share a place with my sister Roma, and Shirley's daughter Marguerite. Richard was the guarantor, and because there were three of us, it was affordable. Roma stayed no more than a month before moving to New York. I think she found the area we lived in dull. She preferred the city, where there was action when she stepped out her apartment door. Jeffrey Meeks, now an orthodontist and the son of Charles and Corina Meeks, moved in with us. When Marguerite left for Harvard a year later and Jeffrey for Jamaica, I rented a one-bedroom apartment and, during my last year in Washington, lived on my own.

After passing the two eight-hour exams that were preconditions for writing my thesis in 1988, I was encouraged by my professors to stay on for an extra year to do the writing. But by now I had decided that Michael was not, to my mind, doing an acceptable job of parenting the children. Parenting was divided between Sarah, Rosie and Nurse. Neither Rosie nor Nurse lived at Washington Close. Sarah was going through a rebellious period but had always been protective of Natasha. I felt the time had come for me to return home and take care of my children, and to see Natasha through her Caribbean Examinations Council exams (CXCs). I knew I was taking a risk and that I might never write my thesis, but Natasha and David had to be my priority. Guilt about leaving them continued to consume me.

Before I left Washington, I sat on Shirley's back porch to discuss how I would re-enter Jamaica. Public opinion was against me. Party leaders felt — and some said as much to me — that even if I had to leave Michael, I should not have done it so publicly. Shirley and I discussed work possibilities and concluded that although it would be difficult for me, I would survive. I knew that returning was the right decision.

In the spring of 1988, I moved back into Hopefield to begin a new, and in some ways the most difficult, phase of my life. No one would employ me for fear that they would upset Michael. By this time Michael's image was far more acceptable to the forces that had once resisted him. He had made several trips to the United States since the election defeat, seeking to repair his image with the US administration. He had spoken to right-wing organisations such as the Heritage Foundation and had met with members of the US congress. A small group of friends in the United States, including Jamaica's lobbyist in Washington, George Dalley, made sure that every time Michael visited he would have the opportunity to discuss issues with critical groups that had been hostile to him in the 1970s. This approach was in keeping with a speech to the party's annual conference in the 1980s that he wanted 'no quarrel.'

Michael and the PNP were returned to power in February 1989, and now there was little to distinguish it from the JLP. Michael was loved by the Bush administration at the time and was honoured when President Bush sent a plane for him to attend a dinner in his honour at the White House. When President Bush was vice-president of the United States and visited Jamaica in the 1970s , his visit had been boycotted by the PNP. How things had changed!

As I tried to settle back into life in Jamaica, I could not find a job. Back in the late 1980s, when others had been too nervous to have anything to do with me, I had been helped by people such as Lorna Gordon Gofton, a feminist and communications expert who employed me anonymously to help with research she was doing for international, regional and local projects, mostly on issues related to gender. Through Leonie Forbes, who was teaching at The Caribbean Mass Communications Institute (CARIMAC), I was given the opportunity to teach modules in communication. Alma Mock Yen was in charge of this area and I appreciated her courage in supporting me at a time when many others would not.

Unfortunatley, this time around was different. I remember being told by Carlton Alexander, one of the critical private sector leaders to whom I had desperately gone for help in finding a job, that no one would believe that I needed to work. Given what I had been to Michael in the 1970s and that I was the mother of his children, said Carlton, surely Michael would find a way to ensure that I would not want for anything. Michael did not see it that way. And anyway, I was proud. I did not want handouts; I wanted to be economically independent. So I continued to look for work on my own — but still without success.

Eventually, in 1990, feeling desperate, I appealed to Michael. Our relationship had by then become what one might call amicable. He sent me to P.J. Patterson and Paul Robertson, as he insisted on distancing himself from this decision. In any case, he told me, of all the cabinet ministers, only Portia Simpson would be willing to work with me. When Portia heard of my dilemma, she consulted with Patterson and Robertson and appointed me as her adviser on gender affairs and subsequently as consultant director for the Bureau of Women's Affairs. I will always be grateful to her, for helping me to regain my self-esteem. She may have saved my life.

My original office was in the Ministry of Welfare under the leadership of Permanent Secretary Alvin McIntosh. He and I had a great relationship and 'Mr Mac' and his staff did everything to make me feel comfortable. When I took over the bureau, my office was at Ripon Road, which also housed the National Insurance Fund. During those years, Portia and I intensified a relationship that had begun in the 1970s. She never criticised me for leaving my marriage. We talked often and openly about the terrible conditions in her inner-city constituency: the violence and lack of social amenities, which obliged women to bathe openly at standpipes and the lack of adequate toilet facilities. Sometimes she would send for me, lock the door to her office, and discuss matters with me about which she was so emotional that tears would come to her eyes.

My assistant at the Bureau was Elaine Rainford, a social worker who had previously been general secretary of the YWCA. Our small team was able to involve everyone, across party lines, in what we were doing. With the help of funding from the Canadian International Development Association (CIDA) and, to a lesser extent, agencies such as the Inter-American Development Bank (IDB) we were able to implement a programme to raise the consciousness of the public sector on gender issues. We created an inter-ministry committee and held training sessions for policymakers to ensure that gender was taken into account in all government's policies and programmes. There was a new buzz in the public sector around gender and simultaneously there were levels of resistance. We initiated seminars with the Administrative Staff College, the body responsible for the training of civil servants. We also carried out practical work such as building and operating a day care centre in Port Antonio and encouraged all ministries to do the same. Our minister, Portia, set the example by setting up a day-care centre in her own ministry.

My work at the Women's Bureau was incredibly fulfilling. We were able to get a great deal of work done in terms of sensitising the bureaucracy to the critical importance of gender roles and responsibilities and the impact of these on policies and programmes. In particular, this period of my life helped me to regain a foothold, personally and professionally. I was determined to make it, if only because Michael had said I couldn't.

By 1990, I had received an invitation from Radcliffe/Harvard to continue my gender research. The Bunting Institute at Radcliffe had been created as a place for female scholars who, for one reason or another, needed to get away in order to complete their academic study. It was the perfect escape for me. I was part of the Distinguished International Visitors Programme, which was funded by the Carnegie Corporation and John Kenneth Galbraith and Catherine Atwater Galbraith. My niece, who had married an African American, was living in Boston, so I had a close relative there. I decided to take leave from the Women's Bureau to pursue academics.

Just before I left for Radcliffe, Michael asked me to come and see him. By now the story was all over Jamaica about his affair. I had learned of it about two years before I left the marriage. At first I had refused to believe it and, of course, Michael had always denied it.

As we sat on Natasha's bed at Hopefield Avenue that day in 1991, Michael said that he wanted to prepare me for the fact that within a year, he would need a divorce in order to remarry. He wouldn't get married while he was prime minister but would wait until he had retired. I knew he would be retiring before the end of the term. I suggested that we not wait, that we deal with the divorce immediately, but I had a condition. Could he find it in his heart to buy a town house and car for Sarah? By now, Sarah was a single head of a household with a family. Michael agreed on the car, but couldn't afford the house.

Later that year, with the divorce final, my relationship with Michael Manley formally came to an end.

In many ways I was relieved, but I was also aware that Michael and I had created two children and that for as long as we lived, we would have joint responsibility for Natasha and David. I promised myself that I would do everything possible to ensure that the children suffered as little hurt as possible over our divorce, and that they would know that we loved them and would always love them. I also felt sadness at giving up Nyumbani, the house in the mountains where both children had been conceived, that we had built so lovingly together.

While at Radcliffe I was supported by Dessima Williams, a former Grenadian ambassador to Washington in Maurice Bishop's regime. We were next-door neighbours in the Harvard

apartments that we lived in right there in Harvard Square. I
hated Boston; the winter depressed me totally. I left the
apartment in the dark and returned in the dark. It was so cold.
As part of my programme at Harvard, I was allowed to invite
scholars to discuss my research on Gender Policy. The team I
selected was Peggy Antrobus, Michael Kauffman who had written
a book on Michael and the 1970s and who understood the
critical importance of gender issues, Dr Lucille Mair, the woman
who was responsible for creating the Women's Bureau in Jamaica
and largely responsible for introducing me to gender issues,
and Locksley Edmondson, whom I had first met when he taught
me International Relations at The University of the West Indies.

In spite of the dark and chilliness of Boston, when Locksley
offered me a fellowship at the Africana Institute, of which he
was the head, at Cornell University in Ithaca, New York, I jumped
at it. And so, in the spring of 1992, I left one cold, dark place
for another. It was a hard time. I missed Jamaica, I missed my
children. I wondered whether I would ever be able to return to
the island. What saved me at Cornell was that for the entire
semester I was the house guest of Locksley and his wife Marcia.
They were wonderful to me, and I became close to them and
fond of their two small children, Magnus and Alicia.

While I was at Cornell, and after my own divorce had
become final, D.K. surprised me one day with news of his divorce.
He called me in my office to tell me he had just left the divorce
courts. I told him I would call him back. I had broken up with
him just before leaving for Cornell — it was one of our many
break-ups, all initiated by me. I looked out to the snow-filled
fields of Cornell and wondered what on earth had propelled

him to go ahead with the divorce. Perhaps it was because he felt me slipping from his grasp. If that was so, it had the desired effect. We resumed our relationship.

I returned to Jamaica without completing my dissertation. It is one of my regrets, but I felt it more important to be with Natasha while she passed her own examinations. I rejoined the Bureau of Women's Affairs, but I had also become interested in reviving my career in radio and began looking for a way to break in again. What I wanted was to combine academics and radio, two of my passions. One day I got a telephone call from Anthony Abrahams, a former tourism minister in a JLP cabinet. I had known Anthony through Shirley and Richard when they were all at Oxford University and shared a flat. Roma and I were living in London at the time, and we would spend weekends with them; Anthony was always happy to have us. Now he had an idea for a new programme, and asked me if I would be one of the regular, volunteer guests to join the weekday discussions on a programme to be called *The Breakfast Club*. But this did not interest me. When he called me back it was to say that Neville James of KLAS-FM radio had suggested that Tony ask me to co-host. Tony and I had lunch and he went out of his way to woo me. It worked. I agreed, although I mentioned my doubts about the programme's longevity. The programme's time slot was 6:00–9:00 a.m., at which time Jamaicans were accustomed to listening to music, not serious discussions. Tony also told me that we would be working in partnership with the radio station on a revenue-share basis, which meant that we had to make money from advertising in order to be paid. He was determined that it could work. I was not convinced, but I decided to give it a try while still working at the Bureau.

We hit the ground running with *The Breakfast Club*. The programme was broadcast live from the Pegasus Hotel in New Kingston every weekday morning. Outside broadcasts took place from time to time in other hotels throughout Jamaica or in corporations. The format was simple. Tony and I were co-hosts and every morning we were joined by two club members drawn from a list of about 20 working in the private sector, the trade unions and academia. D.K. was a regular contributor. Later, we added one or two community leaders. The programme was unique to Jamaica, in that we called experts all over the world to join our discussions. It was, as one person described it, 'a university live on air'. Despite the fact that critics believed Jamaicans would not be interested in intellectual discussion on radio and that the show would have a short shelf life, listeners loved it. We were creating a revolution in radio programming — Tony and I came from different political backgrounds (he was a former cabinet minister, and I was a former prime minister's wife and political activist), and discussed international issues, such as the struggle between the Tutsis and the Hutus in Rwanda, and apartheid in South Africa, as well as social issues such as homophobia. We were proud to be able to bring to the Jamaican people discussions about the living conditions in many of our inner-city areas, and during election time we were on the road covering special events. Occasionally we would broadcast from abroad, once travelling to Trinidad and Tobago, and on another occasion to Florida. The programme had started off targeting people in the top strata of Jamaican society but, increasingly, all social classes began tuning in. It was said that *The Breakfast Club* was not so much a programme as a movement.

Its popularity grew at a time when Jamaicans were increasingly frustrated over their political parties, and more open to discussing issues that transcended tribal lines.

As the programme succeeded, doors opened for me socially and professionally. I began to receive offers of consultancies on gender issues from such organisations as the World Bank, the Inter-American Development Bank and the United Nations Research Institute for Social Development. Many of these consultancies had an impact on policymaking in Jamaica and further assisted me in restoring my image in Jamaican society. This was what I needed to centre myself, to establish a strong reputation of my own. I began to feel part of Jamaica once again, to feel once more that I was making a difference.

I would remain with *The Breakfast Club* for 13 years, leaving in 2004 to begin writing this memoir.

Afterword

In time Michael's attitude softened towards me. It was very important to both of us that the children know that in spite of the end of the relationship, we loved them both. This was at the forefront of all our interactions with each other. He was diagnosed with cancer early in his third term and, as a result, left politics in March 1992. He and Glynne married soon after that, and less than two years later, he was bedridden. He was 73 years old.

Michael worried, he often told me, about how history would assess him. He worried constantly about his legacy. It was important to him that his children recognise and appreciate what he had tried to do for Jamaica, that they should understand his deep concerns about justice and equality. Yet he was relieved that none of them appeared to be interested in going into politics. He knew what it was like to be the child of parents in political life. After all, he had constantly been compared to his own father who he loved dearly – but it was often difficult for him to be his own person as he operated under the shadow of parents who were both formidable in their own right. He did not want that for his children.

As for me, I suppose it was natural in those final months for me to wonder what my life might have been like if I had chosen to stay with Michael, though there was no doubt in my mind that my life was less complex now. I felt a sense of relief as I returned to myself without the encumbrances of political life.

During his long illness and particularly when he became bedridden, David asked Michael to allow me to visit him whenever I desired, so that I could keep him and Natasha up to date on their father's condition. Michael cleared this with Glynne; it was important to him that she was comfortable with the visits. He told me that he didn't like us both being in the room at the same time; he could feel the tension. And so I only visited him when the children were there, and kept track of his health through Joseph, Rachel and Sarah, who were in constant touch with their father. The arrangement was that, when the time came, I would be told so that I could bring Natasha and David — both then in London — home as quickly as possible. Each of the children spent extra time with their father when they could, including David whenever he was home from school in England. Michael knew that he would not live to see his youngest child graduate. In the case of Natasha, she was able to spend months with him on a daily basis during his illness. This was important to her — spending this time with her father.

Three days before Michael passed away, there was a desperate-sounding message on my telephone voice-mail. The voice, which sounded like his, begged me to come and see him: there was something he had to tell me. I rushed to Michael's home as soon as *The Breakfast Club* ended, but just as I was about to climb the stairs to his bedroom, Glynne appeared and told me that she would not allow me to see him. I was so shocked and hurt that I just ran out the door, got into my car and drove off. I guessed that she was in no state to have anyone visit but I was devastated by what she said to me. Later she asked Rosie to talk to me about it. I kept the voice-mail message on my phone for several days and even played it back to Rosie and the children, who all agreed that the voice sounded like his. Yet we knew he was too weak to dial the number, and his nurses later told us that none of them had dialled it for him. I was convinced that the voice was in fact his, what had he wanted to tell me and why had he sounded so conspiratorial and secretive? It is a mystery that I would never solve.

On the day that Michael departed this world, my son and I stood for a while alone by his bedside. David was only 16, and about to do his GCE examinations in England. Michael and I had dreaded this moment since I got pregnant, knowing that because of his age it was possible that David could lose his father while still young. David and I held hands and looked down on this person we loved and thought about how much he had suffered and for how long. I knew Michael had the memory of an elephant and was often unforgiving, but I hoped that now, in his final hours, he had forgiven himself and everyone else — including me. I recalled Michael telling me how frightened he was of death. Joseph called me to tell me he had passed on. I insisted on going on air that morning and immediately after the programme, I joined others at his house. Ashes to ashes, dust to dust, played in my mind as I said goodbye to this great man who so feared the death that was now upon him.

The funeral was held at the largest church that was available, the Roman Catholic cathedral in downtown Kingston. All Michael's children attended — Rachel, Joseph, Sarah, Natasha and David — along with his ex-wives Thelma and myself; Della, his brother Douglas and nephews Norman and Roy. Natasha was so overwhelmed by her father's death that on two occasions she had gone to Heathrow Airport in London to depart for Jamaica, but just couldn't make the trip. Eventually, she found the strength to join us. At the funeral she rallied, and read the Dylan Thomas poem 'Do not go gentle into that dark night'. I was so proud of her as she stood there, tall and confident in her grief and reading the poem as her father would have wanted.

As she read, I remembered how, from early on, Michael and I took her campaigning with us, and that she took her first steps at a Comrade's home in Negril. I remembered how she had often held her clenched fist — the Party's symbol — up on the platforms of PNP rallies. I remembered how overwhelmed she was by the love of the people for her; she was the first and only child born at Jamaica House. She was my baby girl, my feminist pride and joy, who had gone everywhere with me. I just hadn't been able to let her go. She had come a long way, our little girl. Her father would have been proud.

The children were devastated by their father's death and wondered how they would survive without this giant of a man in their lives. A father they could always turn to and somehow he would make everything worthwhile. I was most worried about Natasha and David, who would both return to England where they had no family support. I would not be there with them for what would certainly be an extended period of grieving. Thank God they had each other.

Following the service our congregation, headed by a host of dignitaries, walked the couple of miles to National Heroes Circle where Michael would be buried. The adults and children who lined the streets on either side cheered us along. After Michael's body had been interred, Prime Minister Percival James Patterson invited a number of people to Vale Royal. We had the opportunity to meet and talk with some of the attending dignitaries, including Fidel Castro and Louis Farrakhan. Michael's party supporters said that they couldn't imagine life without him. Many in attendance hailed him as a visionary and a leader who had an international perspective, who had the courage not to shy away from hard decisions. I remember Farrakhan holding David's hands and telling him passionately that spiritually his father's mantle had now been passed to him. David was just 16 years old and couldn't imagine what Minister Farakhan was talking about.

Although Glynne's home was the official mourning home, mine was the informal one. During the days following his death, scores of people passed through, expressing their condolences — and reliving memories of the turbulent 1970s.

Looking back over my life and experiences, I observe patterns. The struggle between powerfulness and powerlessness was played out early between my mother and father, and those conflicts have plagued me since. More than once I have given up my own power for a man of power. I know now that my intense attraction to Michael was in part an attraction to power outside of myself. My entire life with him was about supporting him in what he was doing. I justified this to myself through the work I did on behalf of the PNP Women's Movement but, in the end, it was all about him and his party. When he lost the election in 1980 and reneged on democratic socialism, all I could see was failure; all I could feel was disappointment. Michael was no longer the man that I knew and with whom I had fallen in love.

At the time I became involved with D.K., I thought that he would be the one to lead Jamaica out of its misery. I gave up everything again and followed D.K., my pattern playing itself out yet again. At the time, no one could advise me to do otherwise. No one could tell me that leaving Michael for D.K. was madness. Many tried. I often wonder whether I had a sort of nervous breakdown after the election loss in 1980. In my clinging to D.K., himself a married man still living with his wife, I was a drowning woman reaching for a lifesaver.

I tried to leave D.K. several times over the years, though I always found my way back. At one stage we discussed marriage, but we were never able to commit to this critical step. Today, 26 years after we started seeing each other, we continue to live together. D.K. is very different from my father, different from Michael. With him I had to grow up in a hurry, had to become more independent. Our life together continues to offer up its challenges. Yet I remain.

In the fall of 2007 as I was writing this book, my mother died. My father had passed away in 1976 and largely thanks to Mama, the grieving period was short and not as painful as it might have been. My mother insisted that we get on with our lives. Now, more than 30 years later, her passing has left me deeply traumatized and reflecting on everything she was to me. I began to question my purpose and the extent to which I had projected my feelings onto her and others. After years of doing transformation work, particularly through Landmark Education Corporation it was time for me to take responsibility for my life. As I shared stories with siblings and friends who gathered around following her death, I recognised her life as one of sacrifice for all of us, and we prepared a loving and sensitive celebratory funeral service for her. We gave thanks for all she had done for us. The best way to honour her, we decided, would be to establish the Esmine Anderson Scholarship Fund, which, on an ongoing basis would assist students at the university of the West Indies, of which both Shirley and I are graduates. The funding for the scholarship comes largely from rental of the house that she saved so hard to buy for herself.

I have the strength now to choose what to take from the experience of my mother — her defiance, her integrity. During my journey through public life, I lost my way without knowing it. In finding my way back to myself, I know now, more than ever, that having the courage to speak what is in my heart, to speak my truth, is her most precious legacy to me.

She always prayed that her children would recognise themselves as Children of God. All of us have come to some deep level of spiritual guidance in our lives. The New Thought Spiritual Movement has been particularly useful to me in providing the kind of tools that help me to live an effective life. I now have my own radio discussion programme on air every week-day morning from 6:00–9:00 a.m. The essence of the programme is transformation in keeping with my vision for a society where individuals come to understand the importance of transforming themselves, their relationships, their work place, their communities and their society. I have plans to bring similar programmes to television. I am more at peace than I have ever been in my life. I take responsibility for my life and hold myself accountable for my experiences. The journey with its ups and downs is indeed worth it.

CPSIA information can be obtained at www.ICGtesting.com
Printed in the USA
LVOW01s1323060715

445124LV00025B/490/P